What Others Have Said about Vance Havner:

"Vance Havner used the Word of God like a sword. You pick any one of his books and you could sense the presence and power of the Holy Spirit leaping off those pages."

—Billy Graham

"Vance Havner . . . is imitated, but he will never be duplicated. I rejoice that we have his ministry available to a new generation that is seeking something more than the average Christian life."

—Warren W. Wiersbe

"Vance Havner was one of a kind. His bold proclamation, unique word-play and homespun stories combined to encourage and inspire those who heard him."

—Michael Duduit

"Vance Havner had one of the best pens around. His unique way of expressing time-honored truths was always significant and Spirit blessed."

—Lewis A. Drummond

"Reading Havner always provides fresh insight and understanding about the Christian Life. He never pulled punches or wasted words, but insightfully cut right to the point."

—Bob Dasal

"The last century produced no greater revivalist than Vance Havner."

—Tom Elliff

"Havner speaks with grace, without neglecting the salt, and he does it with conviction and style."

—Frank Pollard

"All of us have quoted Vance Havner . . . his sermons, always pithy, ever relevant and most assuredly convicting."

—Erwin Lutzer

"Havner was a prophet of righteousness and revival."

—Stephen F. Olford

HOLY DESPERATION

FINDING GOD IN YOUR DEEPEST POINT OF NEED

VANCE HAVNER

COMPILED AND EDITED BY DENNIS HESTER

Fort Washington, PA 19034

Holy Desperation
Published by CLC Publications

U.S.A.
P.O. Box 1449, Fort Washington, PA 19034

UNITED KINGDOM
CLC International (UK)
Unit 5, Glendale Avenue, Sandycroft, Flintshire, CH5 2QP

This printing 2020

Compiled and edited by Dennis Hester. The text of this book is from transcribed sermons preached by Vance Havner at the Ben Lippen Conference. A portion of the royalties from this book will go to the Vance Havner Scholarship Fund at Columbia International University.

Printed in the United States of America

ISBN (paperback): 978-1-61958-317-7
ISBN (e-book): 978-1-61958-318-4
Unless otherwise noted, Scripture quotations are from the Holy Bible, King James Version.

Italics in Scripture quotations are the emphasis of the author.
Variations in wording of Scripture are the author's paraphrase.

Contents

Editor's Preface

ARE YOU DESPERATE for a fresh touch from God? Vance Havner reminds us that everyone in the Bible who got a blessing was desperate.

In Chapter 5, "If Any Thirst," Havner says,

> "If any man thirst" is the first requirement here, and that indicates desperation. Thirsting is not just casually wanting a drink of water; thirst is getting so desperate for a drink of water it's all you can think about. And this holy thirst for God is getting to the place where nothing else will satisfy you.
>
> All the way through the Bible, every one of the great heroes of faith were desperate people: Daniel in the lion's den, the Hebrew children in the fiery furnace, Elijah and Isaiah, Mary, Martha, and Lazarus, the disciples in the storm, Jacob at Jabbok, Moses at the Red Sea, David facing Goliath, the four lepers at the gate of Samaria—and so it goes, every one of them on the spot, desperate.

It seems to me that Havner, this exceptional preacher, was desperate and had a holy thirst for God. Therefore, his desperation to please His Lord opened for him heaven's door for some of God's greatest blessings.

Havner was licensed to preach at the age of twelve and ordained at fifteen. He has been called "the most quoted preacher in America" and was a modern-day prophet from pulpit and pen, having written over thirty books. A powerful revivalist, he uses his homespun humor and shares penetrating truths throughout these Bible-centered messages. He spoke with purpose and power, and the Holy Spirit used him to touch those who were desperate for God.

When we feel far from God and need a fresh touch from Him, when we want to obey Him more than anything else, we are becoming desperate. And when we desperately need God and want God more than anything else—we will find Him and be blessed.

My prayer is that from these messages in *Holy Desperation* you will learn how to find God through His Son, Jesus Christ, and be blessed. May God make all of us more desperate for Him!

As much as possible, these printed messages are as Vance Havner spoke them in various churches and Bible conferences throughout his seventy-plus years of ministry. As compiler and editor, I have taken the liberty of clarifying and shortening long introductions and invitations. I have also removed occasional redundancy between messages (like most preachers, Havner used some of his favorite illustrations and examples in multiple sermons).

Otherwise, every effort has been made to allow Havner to speak for himself in these printed messages as he did in his recorded messages. While Havner may have occasionally "chased rabbits" (digressed) in his sermons, even then what he had to say was so unusually witty and filled with wisdom it was worth hearing—and it gives the reader an insight into this remarkable man of God who wanted to be known as "just a preacher."

I thank God that I had the privilege of knowing and spending time with Vance Havner. I treasure the memories of our conversations which were always filled with laughter and encouragement. I never listen to one of his messages or read one of his sermons that I am not convicted and motivated to be a better preacher and servant of our Lord.

If you do not know this man of God and preacher of preachers, I plead with you to get to know him and learn from him. Use his sermons, outlines, quotes, clever one-liners, and pepper his illustrations throughout your sermons for the seasoning of your soul and the souls of your congregation.

Thanks are extended to my friend Anita Barrett for her diligence in helping to transcribe Havner's messages.

Dennis Hester
Compiler and Editor

And the L*ORD* *God formed man of the dust of the ground, and breathed into his nostrils the breath of life; and man became a living soul.*

Genesis 2:7

And when he had said this, he breathed on them, and saith unto them, Receive ye the Holy Ghost.

John 20:22

All scripture is given by inspiration of God and is profitable for doctrine, for reproof, for correction, for instruction in righteousness.

Second Timothy 3:16

1

Are You Out of Breath?

SOME TIME ago, Reader's Digest had an article on deep breathing that said most of us only use part of our lungs when breathing. There is plenty of air around us and more lung space than we use within us, and we ought to make the most of our resources. After all, breathing is pretty important. Everything depends on it. When you quit breathing, you quit, period. You are never more than a few breaths from death and eternity.

We read in Genesis that God made man out of the dust and breathed into his nostrils the breath of life, and man became a living soul. Man is a God-inspired being. We're not just matter. We're living souls. And what makes the difference is the breath of God.

In Job it says, "The spirit of God hath made me, and the breath of the Almighty hath given me life" (Job 33:4). There is ordinary human inspiration in great literature and great music, but the Bible is more than a book; it is breath—the breath of God. I am not interested in all these many theories of inspiration. I believe this is God's Word, not just in spots or wherever it speaks to you, but in its entirety, any time and all the time. All the Scripture is breathed of God.

I heard of a businessman who attended a Bible meeting, but he was not used to such functions. They asked him to read the Scripture. After he had read it, he said, "If there are no corrections or additions, the Scriptures will stand as read." Well, I agree with that!

John 20:22 says that our Lord, after His resurrection, appeared in the midst of the disciples and "he breathed on them." This was a prophetic breathing preceding Pentecost.

Every Christian is God-breathed, for when he is born again, God breathes into him eternal life, and he is indwelt by the Holy Spirit. He is first convicted by the Holy Spirit. He is regenerated by the Holy Spirit. He is indwelt by the Holy Spirit. He is baptized into the body of Christ by the Holy Spirit.

He is also supposed to be filled with the Holy Spirit. That doesn't mean his heart is an empty vessel every morning to be filled up for the day; being filled is a continuous experience. It begins, of course, with an initial experience. Here in John 20:22 we have the breathing of the Holy Spirit for power, the infilling of the Holy Spirit.

The church is God-breathed. It is a heavenly fellowship endued with life from above. All churches are empowered for service and testimony.

Bones, Body, and Breath

Have you read of Ezekiel's vision of the valley of dry bones (Ezekiel 37)? He looked out over that gruesome spectacle, and he was asked, "Can these bones live?" I've felt like asking that question when I've stood up in the pulpit before some congregations! But, all through this chapter, in 37:5, 6, 8, 9, and 10, you have three things: bones, body, and breath.

First of all, he saw just bones. And then the flesh came upon them, and they stood up, but that was not enough. And so, the breath of God had to play upon them. The word for "wind" and the word for "spirit" are the same in Hebrew and Greek, and it's a very interesting thing that it required three things to make a complete organism, in this case.

A church may have the bones of organization and sound theology. It may have the body of a large membership. But if the breath of the Holy Spirit is not on it and in it, then it is only like the church of Sardis—having a name, a reputation, of being alive, when it is really dead (see Rev. 3:1).

And don't forget, Sardis was a very active church—it had a name of being alive. It wasn't about to die; the preacher wasn't about to resign and the roof wasn't about to fall in. They were doing a lot of things around there. They had a name of being alive. But Jesus said, "I've got another name for you."

An undertaker can make a dead man look better than he ever looked while he was living. And some church "experts" can get hold of a church and get it looking pretty good, but the Lord knows the difference. A Christian may have the bones of sound doctrine, and he may have meat on the bones. There may be meat in what he believes. But unless the Spirit of God indwells and fills him, he's still not carrying on an effective ministry.

THE GREATEST NEED TODAY, FOR THE CHURCH AND THE INDIVIDUAL CHRISTIAN, IS BREATH.

A sermon may have the bones of a good outline. It may have the body of good content. But, unless the breath of

God blows on that sermon, it's only "sounding brass, or a tinkling cymbal" (1 Cor. 13:1). I've listened to some sermons that had the bones all right; they were just skeletons. And then, I've heard others that had some meat on them, but you still felt the Spirit wasn't blowing across them.

The greatest need today, for the church and the individual Christian, is breath.

Dr. J.B. Phillips said that the church today is so prosperous, it's fat and out of breath, and so organized, it's muscle-bound. That's a good description of the average church today. And I've visited a lot of churches where they're puffing and blowing and exhaling all the time, without inhaling. A church can't last if it's giving out in ministry all the time without being refilled by the Spirit of God.

When I was a boy, I heard Dr. Wilbur Chapman, a great Presbyterian and quite an effective pastor and evangelist back in the days of D.L. Moody. But he was concerned about the condition of his own heart. He went to F.B. Meyer, that great saint of the Lord, and said, "Why is my Christian experience so intermittent—fluctuating up and down, up and down?"

And Meyer said, "Did you ever try to breathe out three times before you breathed in once?"

The first-aid technique of artificial respiration is used to revive someone when they stop breathing. And the church is also using a lot of artificial respiration today. Sometimes they revive the organism temporarily, and resuscitate the corpse momentarily, but it's not real revival—it's just breathing human breath into a carcass. We have a lot of church "respiration experts" around who make a living blowing ordinary human inspiration into churches that are out of the breath from heaven.

Have you ever watched a song leader trying to get a crowd to sing that didn't have a song down in their heart? That's the hardest work on the face of the earth, trying to pull out a song that's not there. What's down in the well will come up in the bucket. And, when you're trying to bring up what's not down there, you've got a job on your hands. It's a frustrating business—an exercise in futility. And we're spending a lot of time in churches today trying to pull out of hearts what's never been put in them—getting them to exhale in service when they've not inhaled from the blessing of God.

There are two verbs in what I've just read about Jesus over in John 20:22: "And . . . he breathed on them, and saith unto them, Receive ye the Holy Ghost." The Lord must *breathe* into us what He breathes upon us, and we must *receive* it. There is the giving and there is the receiving. Open-endedness is a term we use for this, and the Christian must be open on the godward side all the time. And then in service to others, the Christian must be open on the humanward side, open toward God for strength and open toward others for service.

The Double Experience

If a lake doesn't have any inlet, it's exhausted; and if it doesn't have an outlet, it's stagnant. And, so it is with the Christian experience. The church at Jerusalem had to go through persecution to scatter them throughout the known world, preaching the word. They were in process of stagnation. Jesus said, "Tarry ye" (Luke 24:49), and then he said, "Go ye" (Matt. 28:19), and we need that double experience.

Every Christian heart ought to have a mirror in it in which to look at ourselves. It's not very encouraging, but we need to look once in a while. Isaiah got a reflection of himself when he first saw the Lord, and he said, "Woe is me!" (Isa. 6:5). And then, we need a window in our heart, having seen ourselves and face God as Isaiah did to look out on the needs of this world. You see, we're the salt of the earth, and salt is no good in a saltshaker; it's got to be shaken out before it's effective. A Christian is not a depository of the truth; he's a dispenser of the truth.

Are you having the experience of taking in from God and giving out in blessing?

Now, if I may change horses in the middle of the stream, to another figure from air to water. Jesus said that if we drink of the living water, from within us shall flow rivers of living water. There you have the giving and receiving again. Openness toward God, "let him drink," and openness toward man, "from within him shall flow rivers of living water" (see John 7:37. 38). Are you having the experience of taking in from God and giving out in blessing?

This experience isn't just for preachers. There are some precious laypeople, some of them are old grandmothers, who can tell you something about the inflowing and the outflowing of God's Spirit.

Have you ever seen an electric sign with several of the letters burned out? It makes for terrible reading. Sometimes I meet Christians that are like that. Some of them are out, and some of them are shaky; they've never been plugged into the divine power of God or else they're not living in close fellowship with God. The book of the Acts of the Apostles is simply a record of the outflow and overflow of the inflow from the Spirit of God. That's all there is. All is vain unless the Spirit of the Holy One comes in.

Not Evangelistic Efforts, but Revival

I've been traveling over this country for a long time, trying to preach that what the church needs today is not evangelistic effort so much as, first of all, to have a real revival that will make them evangelistic. Now, when you've really had revival, you'll be evangelistic, you'll be missionary.

But I'm afraid we've got the cart before the horse today. We hear an awful lot about evangelism. I've been in nearly every one of our Southern Baptist churches where they have a convention and an evangelistic conference. And I've said again and again, we're wasting our time and money trying to get people to do something when they're not ready to serve because they've not been revived, and they aren't living in fellowship with God.

The last word of Jesus to the church was not the Great Commission; it was "Repent!" Jesus called five of the seven churches in the book of Revelation to repentance.

J. Edwin Orr, who has written so many books and has had a term of service for God, has a book that I treasure, and it is entitled, *The Church Must First Repent.* You don't hear repentance preached about much today. I tell preachers, "Go home and preach a series of sermons on the seven churches (see Rev. 1–3). You'll find your church somewhere in that group."

Your congregation will see themselves in those seven churches—though you may have to put two or three of them together to get a composite picture of your church. And there may be a deacon in your church who's not living right, who will object to or be offended by the truth.

I heard of a preacher who said the deacon told him that he was preaching too much hell and judgment, and he ought to preach on love.

"All right," he said, "I will." The next Sunday, he preached on, "Thou shalt love the Lord, thy God," and that night, "Thou shalt love thy neighbor as thyself," and the next Sunday, "Husbands, love your wives and don't love some other man's wife."

After that series of sermons on love, the deacon came up and said, "Preacher, I'd just about as soon you'd go back to preaching on hell!"

If we'll preach the Word, we'll get close to where people live. We're seeing a lot of good things today, but we are not having a real revival because the average church is not repentant. Some have left their first love, like Ephesus, and others have gotten tied up with Balaam and Jezebel. Others are dead like Sardis, some are lukewarm like Laodicea, and they will not repent. The average church is like a lung with only a few cells breathing, a lung full of pneumonia and only a few active cells.

And then there is extremism, "trendism," and emotionalism that the church gets carried away with. Any movement that makes the Holy Spirit the figurehead, as F.B. Meyer said a long time ago, is eccentric; it is off-center; for the business of the Holy Spirit is to magnify Jesus Christ. "He shall testify of me" (John 15:26). The passage that woke me up about being filled with the Holy Spirit was what John said in 7:37–39. If you read through that passage, you'll find the Holy Spirit is not the main one in that picture. "But, this spake he of the Spirit, which they that believe on him should receive: for the Holy Ghost was not yet given; because that Jesus was not yet glorified" (John 7:39).

I don't believe God is going to fill anybody with the Holy Spirit until the purpose of their heart is to glorify Jesus and to glorify God. That's the business of the Holy Spirit. And there are many hungry-hearted preachers and Christians in general seeking a deeper experience of God.

Now, the devil is never any smarter than when he gets people so scared of the filling of the Holy Spirit or whatever you want to call it, that you're scared of the Holy Spirit altogether. After all, there is such a thing as being filled with the Holy Spirit, and many times it is an experience subsequent to regeneration.

Down through the ages, some of the greatest men God has ever used were those that were saved and came through a subsequent experience when they entered into the fullness of what God had for them. We must be careful not to be so scared of getting out on a limb that we never get up the tree. There's a real harm, there's serious danger there. So, for fear of the falls, don't miss the tree.

Spiritual Emphysema

And so, we go along, we're supposed to have the Spirit breathed into us, but the average Christian today has got emphysema, going along gasping all the time for breath. Have you got emphysema, spiritual emphysema? A lot of folks have, and you can't take care of this by just an occasional revival.

I believe in revival, but I think we ought to talk about "vival" instead of "revival." And, what I mean by "vival" is just normal New Testament Christianity. I think revival can be misleading. A lot of people have the idea it's perfectly natural for the saints all to backslide every year and have to call in a preacher every six months to wake them up again. Now, that's not the teaching of the New Testament, because you're supposed to be filled with the Holy Spirit all the time, in any season of the year.

At Old Corinth church in Hickory, NC, where I grew up, we used to have our so-called revival the last week in July. We couldn't have it any other time. That was a set time for the revival. Anybody that wanted to get saved any other time had a pretty rough time of it. They'd have to wait until the last week in July. And we'd have a great time that week. I'm not discounting it; we had a glorious time. The Methodists had their meeting the next week and most of us went over there. My grandmother shouted her way through both meetings. She got just tuned up good in the Baptist meeting and went over to the Methodist, and that's fine. But you can't live on an occasional spasmodic revival.

No Revival without Repentance

The purpose of the New Testament epistles was to develop holy, healthy Christians, and when you're a healthy Christian, you'll be evangelistic, and you'll be missionary, and you'll be a tither, and you'll be everything else you ought to be.

Revival must come, and this has to do with the people of God, not with unbelievers. There can be no revival unless there's repentance, and there can be no repentance till the people of God get down on their knees. You see, we must get out into the world, anybody knows that.

Jesus said, "As thou hast sent me into the world, even so have I also sent them into the world" (John 17:18). But we're trying to send a lot of people not ready to go out there.

They're not ready to go into the world, not till they've been straightened out in their own living before God. This is what I mean by talking about a deep breathing exercise. We're trying to get people to breathe out what's not been breathed in.

I used to read so many books on the subject "How to be filled with the Spirit." Some had four steps, five steps, six steps, seven steps in order to be filled with the spirit and had me stepping all the time. Just as we physically draw short breaths with only a portion of our lungs, so as Christians, we draw just little gasps of divine power, especially in an emergency, instead of a deep daily inhalation of the power of God, as we're supposed to.

A verse that ought to be hung up over all our churches is "So they that are in the flesh cannot please God" (Rom. 8:8). You cannot teach a Sunday School class to the glory of God "in the flesh." Sometimes church committees appoint a lawyer to teach a Bible class just because he's a good talker. But the Bible nowhere says that is a qualification for teaching the Bible. Unless he's filled with the Spirit, he's not qualified.

Just because a man's a banker doesn't qualify him to be church treasurer. He must be "filled with the Spirit." Somebody said, in order to breathe like you ought to; you must first exhale the foul air from your lungs and then breathe in the fresh air. Get rid of the sin in your life.

Old Lynn Broughton, who used to be the pastor at Baptist Tabernacle, got in a meeting of another denomination because he was concerned about this matter of being "filled with the Spirit." He went down to the front, preacher that he was. And folks said, "Well, do you feel any different?" and he said, "I didn't go up there for feeling. I went up there for filling."

The feeling is a secondary matter altogether. You'll get whatever you need. "And God is able to make all grace abound toward you; that ye, always having all sufficiency in all things, may abound to every good work" (2 Cor. 9:8). I've got that verse on my table at home where I turn on the light first thing of a morning. "God is able to make all grace abound."

THE GREATEST BLESSINGS GO TO DESPERATE PEOPLE.

When I was pastor of the First Baptist Church in Charleston, South Carolina, back in 1934–1939, I was greatly concerned about preaching and living in the "fullness of God's spirit." I wanted to be totally surrendered to God and completely filled and led by His Spirit. And, I would sit in my room, late at night, and think about this subject.

I went to see one of my church members, old Granny Russell, who was a saint of the Lord. She gave me a book called, *Deeper Experiences of Famous Christians* by James Gilchrist Lawson. I went to my room that night and I couldn't go to sleep till I had read it, and then I couldn't go to sleep because I had read it. And, I got under conviction about being filled with His Spirit, but I was trying to wake myself up with a spiritual experience to suit me.

I had to come to the Lord based on John 7:37-39, "If any man thirsts." Now, there's a difference between thirsting and just wanting a drink of water. Have you ever thirsted for the fullness of God in your life? When you thirst, nothing is going to satisfy you but water, and that's all you can think about. And, when you get to a point of holy desperation, when that's all that you're concerned about, God will bless you, fill you, and use you.

The greatest blessings go to desperate people. Come to Jesus, drink, receive, and then believe that you have received (see Mark 11:24), and then from within you will flow rivers of living water. That's as simple as Jesus made it, and that's simple enough. Come and drink and receive.

If you have a thirst in your heart for what you don't have and a thirst for only what God can give you, you can be filled. Only those who are willing to empty themselves can be filled with the breath, the Spirit, and the presence of God.

At the same time came the disciples unto Jesus, saying, Who is the greatest in the kingdom of heaven? And Jesus called a little child unto him, and set him in the midst of them, And said, Verily I say unto you, Except ye be converted, and become as little children, ye shall not enter into the kingdom of heaven.

Matthew 18:1–3

2

Have You Lost the Wonder?

GYPSY SMITH, the great evangelist, died in true "gypsy" tradition—on a journey in his eighty-seventh year. He was called to preach as a lad, sang and preached the gospel around the world. He was simple, original, and colorful. He used to say, "I was born in a field. Don't put me in a flowerpot." Somebody told him he ought to take vocal lessons, and learn how to sing from his diaphragm. He said he didn't want to sing from his diaphragm, he wanted to sing from his heart.

When he started out as a lad to preach, he didn't have much education. He said some of the Bible words were too big for him. He said the way he worked, he'd read till he saw one of those big words coming, and then he'd stop right on this side and make a few remarks and then start reading on the other side.

Gypsy was once asked: "What is the secret of the freshness of your ministry, way into your eighties?" And he said, "I have never lost the wonder."

A good question for a Christian to ask from time to time is, "Have I lost the wonder?"

I heard Gypsy speak in Stonybrook, New York, just before he died, and he hadn't lost the wonder. A preacher ought to have the mind of a scholar, the heart of a child, and the hide of a rhinoceros. The problem is how to toughen your hide without hardening your heart. Gypsy had the heart of a child. He never lost the wonder.

I think this is one thing our Lord tried to explain to his disciples in Matthew 18:1–6.

> At the same time came the disciples unto Jesus, saying, who is the greatest in the kingdom of heaven? And Jesus called a little child unto him, and set him in the midst of them, and said, Verily I say unto you, Except ye be converted, and become little children, ye shall not enter into the kingdom of heaven. Whosoever therefore shall humble himself as this little child, the same is greatest in the kingdom of heaven. And whoso shall receive one such little child in my name receiveth me. But whoso shall offend one of these little ones which believe in me, it were better for him that a millstone were hanged about his neck, and that he were drowned in the depth of the sea.

Children have not lost the wonder. They have not been here long enough to get used to it. They still have a sense of surprise. Anything can happen. Everything is new. At four, you have all the questions, and at eighteen, you have all the answers.

With a child, every turn of the road may hold some glad discovery, and the commonest humdrum day is glorified by the glamour of imagination. Everything with a child is one-quarter fact and three-quarters fantasy, and that makes for interesting living. But, all too soon, and sooner now than ever, they lose the wonder.

The Magic of Childhood

The Saturday Evening Post recently carried an article on what happened to the magic of childhood. It's high time somebody asked it, because youngsters become cynical, sophisticated old men and women before they're out of their teens. We're in the TV age. We've seen everything, heard everything. I wonder what it would take to surprise anybody anymore.

I preached in Indiana some time ago in Mennonite country, where I saw this motto: "We are too soon old and too late smart." How true that is. And yet, we also get smart too soon, and we lose the wonder. Well, the young people are not entirely to blame. We old folks don't have much time to wonder anymore, to meditate and reflect.

I remember when President Teddy Roosevelt went to South America on a hunting trip when he was approaching sixty years of age. The trip practically killed him. He said, "It's my last chance to be a boy." People who knew Theodore Roosevelt always remembered there was a perennial boy in him.

Today, we get over not only childhood, but the spirit of it, all too soon. In my boyhood, we didn't go around saying, "I'm bored; there's nothing to do." (Of course, our fathers always saw to it that there was something to do!) Still, we had time to do nothing sometimes, too, and we often found the times we did nothing were as important as the times we did something.

There was time to be still, to walk in the woods, to sit and meditate before an open fire. I don't think anybody ever thought of anything worth thinking about while looking at a steam radiator. There's something about an open fire.

The Bible says Isaac meditated. Now, if Isaac took off across the fields today meditating, people would say, "Poor Isaac. I was afraid he was coming to that." But Isaac meditated. Today, everything is organized, supervised, planned, programmed, and correlated. You don't just walk now. It must be an organized hike.

I'm a bird watcher. But nowadays you're not just an ordinary bird watcher—you have to join a club and keep records and all that sort of thing, which I never do. You lose the wonder of it in the work of it.

This can happen to Christians as they work in the church. What was meant to be a life of faith, of working by love, becomes highly organized religious activity. The Thessalonian work of faith, and labor of love, and patience of hope, just becomes the Ephesian work of labor and patience, period—because you lose the wonder.

Three Kinds of People

Now, in the light of the text, there are three kinds of people. First, there are *children.* "Jesus took a little child and set him in the midst of them." I've never heard a sermon from this text, and the silence is profound. I think some Christians would be more comfortable if the Lord had used a business tycoon or a scholar or a popular hero for his model. But Jesus puts a little child in the midst of his disciples and upsets our standard, because it's very disconcerting to us adults who like to act as if wisdom would die with us.

Then there are not only children, but the *childish.* Look at Matthew 11:16–19:

> But whereunto shall I liken this generation? It is like unto children sitting in the markets, and calling unto

> their fellows, and saying, we have piped unto you, and ye have not danced; we have mourned unto you, and ye have not lamented. For John came neither eating nor drinking, and they say, He hath a devil. The son of man came eating and drinking, and they say, behold a man gluttonous, and a winebibber, a friend of publicans and sinners. But wisdom is justified of her children.

What a description of this generation! John the Baptist came fasting, and Jesus came feasting, and they called John a demoniac and Jesus a glutton. Nothing suited them. They were like spoiled children who've had too many toys.

Today, our churches are filled with spoiled "adults." They've been petted and pampered and no kind of preaching pleases them. If the wrath of God is preached, the minister is too severe. If the love of God is proclaimed, he's too sentimental. If he speaks in a low tone of voice, he's dull. If he speaks in a loud voice, he's deafening. If he stands still, he's a statue. If he moves around, he's a sensationalist.

That used to bother me a lot until I learned how to identify these children of the marketplace. They play, they pipe, they play a wedding, they mourn, they play funeral; and it looks real, but it's all make-believe. And we play church just like that.

I was invited to Fremont Temple in Boston some time ago for an evangelistic conference, and the pastor said, "We're worried about playing church." Well, I've heard that many times before, but what a common thing it is today to play at it. Our Lord called it play-acting, or *hypocrisy*; they are spiritual babies who won't grow up.

The apostle Paul experienced the same problem in the church in his day. He said, "And I, brethren, could not speak unto you as unto spiritual, but as unto carnal, even as unto babes in Christ. I have fed you with milk, and not with meat: for hitherto ye were not able to bear it, neither yet now are ye able" (1 Cor. 3:1–2).

We have overgrown babies who have become such as have need of milk but not of meat, 150- and 200-pound "church babies" who keep the pastor busy running around with a milk bottle when they ought to have been on meat a long time ago. And then, when they call a new pastor, they say, "I don't like him. He changed my formula." They're a headache and a heartache to any pastor, pouting and selfish—to whom John the Baptist would be only a demoniac and Jesus a glutton.

The third kind of person appears when we have genuine revival—church members quit being childish and become *childlike*. You can call it anything else you want to, but that's it. Here are the keys to the kingdom: conversion and childlikeness. Apostle Paul says,

> That we henceforth be no more children, tossed to and fro, and carried about with every wind of doctrine, by the sleight of men, and cunning craftiness, whereby they lie in wait to deceive; But speaking the truth in love, may grow up into him in all things, which is the head, even Christ. (Eph. 4:14–15)

When we were children, we spoke and understood and thought as children, but we ought to grow up (see 1 Cor. 13:11). We're not to remain babes in Christ, but grow in grace. But, in order to be a childlike Christian, there isn't so much to learn, as there is to unlearn. Because, this secret has been kept from the wise and prudent and revealed unto babes.

A childlike Christian has not lost the sense of wonder. There ought to be about every child of God an expectancy, a sense of surprise, believing that God not only can but will work a miracle. We don't look for miracles. We don't see many. We pray for rain, and we don't take our umbrellas. This is my Father's world. Anything can happen. The happiest fellow in this world is a young Christian before he's met too many Bible scholars.

Despising Our Youth

Some time ago in meetings out in Kansas City, I had the privilege for two weeks of talking to pastors and evangelists, and we had a fine bunch of Australian Baptist preachers there. Oh, what a glorious two weeks at the breakfasts each morning! And one of these fine young preachers said, "Brother Havner, I'm beginning to think that when Paul said to Timothy, 'Let no man despise thy youth', there's another application—we can despise our own youth."

We can reach that sad state when we look down with scorn on our earlier years when we started out all aglow with our first love, but the spiritual honeymoon has become grim reality, and it has smothered our zeal.

Do you remember you loved the Lord and you loved the Bible, and you didn't know any better than to want to tell everybody? You were like a country boy coming to town, like a spiritual yokel maybe, but these sedate souls resting in Zion may have resented your zeal.

But then you grew up, and you became educated and established and experienced, and now you look with common dissension, even distaste, on these brash young Christians like you were once. And you say to the young zealot, "Oh, yes, I used to expect miracles, but I got over it, and you will, too."

I see these faces in preachers' meetings sometimes and evangelistic conferences, and the glow is gone. They look irritated when some young Timothy comes along who reminds them of better days that they once had.

I was in Richmond, Virginia, for a conference, and there was a young man who joined the church on Sunday—a brand new Christian. He came every night to the meetings. He didn't know any better. Some of the deacons didn't come to the meetings, but he did. And, as I watched this young Christian, I found myself praying, "Lord, don't let him catch on. Don't let him see these absent deacons."

IF YOU HAVE LOST THAT GLOW THAT YOU ONCE HAD, THERE'S A PRICE TO PAY TO REGAIN IT.

I was out in Riverside, California, at the First Church and met an old boy out there who had grown up in my home community in Catawba County, a veteran of the First World War. He'd been a bad boy, but his mother kept praying, and God saved him.

He lived out there on the edge of town. He brought his family every night. He was a working man, and it was a hard thing to get them there on time. One night he came up to me after the service and said, "Brother Havner, there's just one question I want to ask you. Where are these folks who've been Christians a long time; why are they not at this meeting?"

I swallowed and cleared my throat a couple of times and looked at him. What would you have said? I didn't want to say, "Well, you'll get over it." I didn't want to say, "They used to come, too, but they despise their youth now."

Nothing does me more good than a brand new Christian. I heard of one "old boy" down in Louisiana who had had such a profound conversion to our Lord when he was saved, his parents thought he was crazy and sent him to a psychiatrist.

The psychiatrist asked him, "Where were you born?"

"Well," he said, "I've been born twice. Which time are you talking about?"

The psychiatrist cleared his throat and asked, "Your father's name, please."

"Well," he said, "I've got a heavenly Father and an earthly father. Which one are you talking about?"

The psychiatrist said, "Where is your home?"

He said, "I've got a heavenly home and an earthly home. Which one are you talking about?"

And, you know, by the time that young Christian's appointment with the psychiatrist was over, they had to send the psychiatrist to a psychiatrist!

Let me tell you, brother, if you have lost that glow that you once had, there's a price to pay to regain it. It will humble you and shatter your complacency, but it's worth it to have your youth renewed as the eagles.

There are some Christians, even some preachers, who have lost the wonder of the Christian life. They pray prayers that have no meaning and preach sermons that have no passion. The salt has lost its savor and it's good for nothing but to be trodden underfoot; insipid, flat, tasteless (see Matt. 5:13).

There ought to be something about our Christianity to smack the lips over. There ought to be a taste and a zest and a relish. I've seen more cheerful faces on iodine bottles than I've seen on some saints over America. Where is the blessedness I knew when first I loved?

At the church at Ephesus, the trouble wasn't false doctrine; it wasn't worldliness. They weren't playing bingo in the basement. They were still sound in doctrine. But you can believe the truth and stand for the truth, and yet in the very activities of the truth you can get over being gripped by the truth so you live in unfelt truth. You can work in the bakery till you lose your taste for the bread. And, it was old Baxter who said, "Many a tailor goes in rags that maketh costly clothes for others, and many a cook scarcely licks his fingers when he hath dressed for others the most costly dishes." Oh, what a besetting ailment that is! The salt loses its taste.

I used to think losing your first love meant you were a confirmed backslider and you'd quit praying and reading your Bible and going to church. Oh, no. You can be in the middle of church work, teaching a Sunday School class, backsliding with a Bible under your arm, leaving your first love.

Think about the Old Testament character Samson, who found himself with shaven head, bound, blind, and grinding, and saying, "I'll shake myself. I'll go through the old calisthenics," but the power was gone, Samson was bound to a treadmill.

You get into the place where it's a battle of wits and a bustle of works, and if you've lost the wonder, you might as well stop the work. Nothing under the sun can be as dry and flat and tedious and exhausting as religious work without the wonder.

No wonder some people dread going to church. No wonder they're bored with the sermons. No wonder the

Sunday School lesson puts them to sleep. We grow weary in well doing. Singing in the choir becomes a chore. Church visiting becomes drudgery. We sing, "I stand amazed in the presence of Jesus . . . and wonder how He could love me." But this generation wants to be amused and entertained instead of edified.

Some years ago, on a train crossing the continent, everybody was unhappy. It was before air conditioning, and it was a stuffy coach. Everybody was miserable except for one man over by a window, and he was having the time of his life. Every once in a while, he'd look out at the passing scene and say, "Wonderful, wonderful."

Finally, somebody could take it no longer and went over and said, "My friend, the rest of us are miserable, and you're having the time of your life. Can you tell us why you keep saying 'wonderful'?"

He said, "I was a blind man until a few weeks ago, and then a great doctor restored my sight. And, what is perfectly commonplace to you is out of this world for me."

My friend, if the Great Physician has opened your eyes; if you've been to the pool of Siloam and have come back seeing; if you've had a touch and no longer see men as trees walking; if all that has happened to you, why shouldn't you make your way through this poor world singing,

> Wonderful, wonderful, Jesus is to me;
> Prince of peace, counselor, mighty God is He,
> saving me and keeping me from all sin and shame.
> Wonderful is my Redeemer Praise His Name.[1]

We need to remember our conversion and become as little children again. G. Campbell Morgan says, "Begin again as though you'd never known Him." And, with all the simplicity of a little child, call it what you want: first love, joy of salvation, victorious life, and revival. The secret of a growing, glowing Christian experience is to be able to say with Gypsy Smith, "I've never lost the wonder."

A few summers ago, I was in a Bible conference where Billy Graham came up on Sunday morning and sat on the platform behind me while I tried to preach about this subject. And after it was over, he leaned over to me and said, "That was for me."

And as we walked out to lunch, he said, "I get the team together once in a while and tell them, 'If we ever get over this, we're sunk.' Organization, all the rest of it won't mean a thing if we, as you put it, lose the wonder."

Then I went up to Minneapolis to the Billy Graham headquarters. Billy said to me, "Somebody told me the other day you said every preacher ought to be converted again at forty." He was around forty then. And he said, "I've been thinking it over, and I'm sure we do."

A couple of summers ago, I preached at old Corinth Baptist Church near Hickory, North Carolina, where I grew up. And then I slipped back to the little house where I had grown up. It still stands there today. You can sit on the front porch at night and see the lights of five little towns in the mountains on the west.

Everybody else had gone to bed, and I sat alone on the front porch and rocked in the old rocking chair, rocked as I had as a little boy.

I'd been listening to a lot of experts, soaking up a lot of information, and reading a lot of new books about relevance and dialogue and communication, and "neo-" this and that.

I just had to get the taste of it out of my mouth. And as I sat there, I felt like praying,

> Backward, turn backward, O Time, in your flight,
> Make me a child again just for tonight![2]

I wanted to forget all that I'd learned. I wanted to sing as best I could with such a cracked voice,

> I love Thee because Thou hast first loved me
> and purchased my pardon on Calvary's tree;
> I love Thee for wearing the thorns on Thy brow;
> If ever I loved Thee, my Jesus, 'tis now.[3]

I wanted to go back to Sunday School and sing, "Jesus loves me, this I know, for the Bible tells me so." I needed conversion and childlikeness.

For those of us who know the Word and do the work, but who have lost the wonder, conversion and childlikeness is a must.

But, of the times and the seasons, brethren, ye have no need that I write unto you. For yourselves know perfectly that the day of the Lord so cometh as a thief in the night. For when they shall say, Peace and safety; then sudden destruction cometh upon them, as travail upon a woman with child; and they shall not escape. But ye, brethren, are not in darkness, that that day should overtake you as a thief. Ye are all the children of light, and the children of the day: we are not of the night, nor of darkness. Therefore let us not sleep, as do others; but let us watch and be sober. For they that sleep, sleep in the night; and they that be drunken are drunken in the night. But let us, who are of the day, be sober, putting on the breastplate of faith and love; and for a helmet, the hope of salvation. For God hath not appointed us to wrath, but to obtain salvation by our Lord Jesus Christ, Who died for us, that, whether we wake or sleep, we should live together with him. Wherefore comfort yourselves together, and edify one another, even as also ye do.

First Thessalonians 5:1–11

3

Getting Used to the Dark

YEARS AGO, while attending a booksellers' convention in Chicago, Frank Boggs, the singer, took me out to supper to one of these restaurants below the street level. Whoever operated it must have loved darkness rather than light. I stumbled into that dim dungeon and fumbled for the chair and mumbled that I needed a flashlight to read the menu.

When the food came, I ate it by faith and not by sight. But gradually, you know how it is, you sit around a while in a dark place and you can begin to be able to identify various objects. And, Frank knew what was going through my mind, and he said, "Isn't it strange how you get used to the dark?"

And I said, "Brother, you've given me a sermon subject," and I've been preaching that one ever since.

We are told in that remarkable translation of Ephesians 6:12, "For we wrestle not against flesh and blood, but against principalities, against powers, against the rulers of the darkness of this world, against spiritual wickedness in high places." One reason we Christians get into so much trouble and make so many mistakes is we don't know what we're up against and what we're dealing with.

I heard of a fellow who had a little dog who was always getting in a fight and always getting licked. Somebody said, "He's not much of a fighter, is he?" And the fellow said, "Oh yeah he's a good fighter, just a poor judge of dogs." So, when we don't judge the dog, we're headed for trouble.

WE'VE NEVER HAD MORE DARKNESS THAN WE HAVE NOW.

The closing of this age is dominated by the powers of darkness. The night is far spent, and men loved the darkness, and they still do, rather than light. We've never had more light, more artificial light than we have now. We've never had more darkness than we have now.

Modern man is able to turn on nuclear brilliance that out-dazzles the sun, but left to himself, the average poor lost mortal is just a wandering star for whom is reserved the blackness of darkness forever. The depths of modern depravity are too vile for any word in our vocabulary.

I heard of a faithful old preacher who preached a great message on the depravity of the human heart. One of his listeners said to him, "I just can't swallow this depravity you've been preaching about."

"Well," the preacher said, "you don't have to swallow it. It's already in you." So, whether we like it or not, we've got it.

I used to say, "Civilization is going to the dogs," but I don't do that anymore, out of respect for the dogs. The putrefaction of the carcass of civilization is waiting for the vultures of judgment. This is not peculiar to skid row, because some of the top racketeers are morally among the pigs, although they may be dressed quite adequately for some other kind of society.

A Subtle Brainwashing Process

I believe the two greatest perils that God's people, the church at large, and people in particular, face is getting used to the dark and getting used to the light. Both are dangerous. We are in the midst of a slow, sinister, subtle brainwashing process that is gradually desensitizing us to evil. Little by little, sin is made to appear less sinful until the light within us becomes darkness, and how great is that darkness? We get used to it; we get acclimated.

It was Lucille Ball who said, "I'm shocked, because I'm not shocked." Now, if she can say that, it seems to me a lot of church members ought to wake up along that line. We accept the literature and the music and the art and the lifestyle of this age without any inner or outer protest, although we're to hate evil and abhor evil and abstain from every appearance of evil.

I heard of an Irishman who came over here and worked for a year, then his wife came over to join him. She said, "Don't these folks talk funny over here?"

He said, "You ought to have heard them a year ago when I came over here."

You can tell how we've been homogenized in the last few years by the new words we use to describe sins that are so prevalent today; adultery is known as free love and the drunkard is a respectable alcoholic. We're trying to mop up the floor while leaving the faucet running. That never has worked and never will.

And then, of course, we have the murderer, and we say, "Well, he just got off to a poor start as a kid. He pushed his oatmeal dish off the table as a baby, then grew up and pushed his wife off Brooklyn Bridge," and the whole thing was just a continuation.

What are we going to do about these folks who are writing all these masterpieces on how to handle Junior and what makes Junior act like he does?

Junior bit the meter man,
    Junior kicked the cook;
Junior's anti-social now
    (according to the book).
Junior smashed the clock and lamp;
    Junior hacked the tree.
(Destructive trends are treated
    in chapters two and three.)
Junior threw his milk at Mom;
    Junior screamed for more.
(Notes on self-assertiveness
    are found in chapter four.)
Junior tossed his shoes and socks
    out into the rain,
(Negation, that, and normal—
    disregard the stain.)
Junior got in Grandpop's room,
    tore up his fishing line.
That's to gain attention
    (see page 89).
Grandpop seized a slipper
    and yanked Junior 'cross his knee,
(Grandpop hasn't read a book
    since 1893.)[1]

I think we ought to reinstate Grandpop today. I don't believe in pushing all of the elders off to an old folk's home, because we need them very seriously at the present time.

We Should Be Different from the World

We learn to laugh at the Puritanism of our earlier years, when this was wrong and that was wrong, but remember in *Pilgrim's Progress* when Christian and Faithful were at Vanity Fair? That was a strange place for those dear souls to be passing through. There wasn't any way that crowd could get along with them. And it says when the folks who ran the fair saw the apparel and heard the speech of the two pilgrims, they seemed as barbarians to each other.

You can explain it away as much as you want to, but there's not that kind of difference today. The average church member isn't shocking the world, because we get along too well. We're too much alike. Tragedy becomes comedy, tolerance, acceptance, and peaceful coexistence. We get used to the dark. Black and white have been smudged into an indefinite gray.

Dr. Jowett (John Henry Jowett, 1864–1923) once said to a group of preachers, "We preachers are tempted to leave our noontide lights behind us in the study, to move about with a dark lantern which we can manipulate to suit our company." We pay the tribute of the smile to the fashionable joke, easy tolerance to ambiguous pleasures. We soften everything to a comfortable acquiescence. We seek to be all things to all men to win some. We're the victims of illicit compromise.

There's nothing distinctive about our character. We wear a business suit when we mix with the businessmen of our congregation. Maybe that big difference that's come over us is why the old preachers are "gone but not forgotten." And, the trouble with us today is we're forgotten but not gone.

I once heard Billy Graham make a confession (I admire him for making it; some folks would be on their guard about their reputation, so they wouldn't be honest enough to be forthright about their faults). He said, "I heard Kenneth Cansler preach the other day on worldliness, and I got under conviction, and I've got to do something about what he talked about." He added, "I find myself laughing at things on television that I wouldn't have laughed at ten years ago, and I've got to do something about it." I know what he was talking about.

I like to watch tennis tournaments on TV. Some of the best tournaments are on Sunday afternoon—all afternoon—and I generally watch them. You wouldn't go to hell for looking at things like that, but as I sat there one afternoon, a voice, not my own, said, *You're preaching tonight to people who are standing between life and death, between heaven and hell, and there's a better way to get ready for it than what you're doing now.*

So it's goodbye to Sunday afternoon tennis tournaments! I don't care who wins, anyhow. What difference does it make?

I'm in a different church nearly every Sunday. And all through these years I've asked God to help me to say the thing that's most worth saying. Sometimes I meet with the choir, and they come out sometimes giggling. I walk into the pulpit and find myself saying, "Here we go again, Lord."

And then the voice speaks to me and says, *But who are you to go strutting into the pulpit in your own self-assurance, when you ought always to go in as though it were the first time, as though it might be the best time, and as though it could be the last time?*

You give me a bunch of folks on Sunday morning who will attend church in that kind of a mood, you're likely to have a revival by twelve o'clock.

THERE ARE SOME THINGS WE HAVE NO BUSINESS EVER GETTING USED TO.

I think about Jim Elliott, who died a martyr to the cause of Christ in South America. He said, "A friend of mine invited me over to his house to watch television, and God spoke to me with Psalm 119:37: "Turn away mine eyes from beholding vanity." That's a good verse to hang on the TV.

The Saturday Review is not a church paper. It's a secular paper. But the other day, it said, "The desensitization of 20th century man is more than a danger to the general safety. There are some things we have no business ever getting used to." I think that's well said. Don't get used to the dark. And the worst of it is, we're not aware of it. God put us here not to get used to it, but to walk in the light.

Getting Used to the Light

We have gotten used to the dark, but we can also get used to the light. Well, how in the world would that be a danger? That's what Jesus said, when he spoke to his hometown folks. He was born in Bethlehem and grew up in Nazareth, but He left there to live in Capernaum, that the scripture might be fulfilled which said, "The people which sat in darkness saw great light; and to them which sat in the region and shadow of death light is sprung up" (Matt. 4:16).

You would've thought they would've welcomed the Son of God. They were nice people. They didn't treat Him like they did at Jerusalem. At least, they didn't crucify Him. But they just didn't repent. And he said,

> And thou, Capernaum, which art exalted unto heaven, shalt be brought down to hell: for if the mighty works, which have been done in thee, had been done in Sodom, it would have remained until this day. But I say unto you, That it shall be more tolerable for the land of Sodom in the day of judgment, than for thee. (Matt. 11:23, 24)

What causes us to get into such a fix? He told us in that same chapter in Matthew, "You're like children playing in the marketplace. You play funeral, nobody cries; you play wedding, nobody laughs. And that's the way it was—John the Baptist came, and they didn't like him, he was so serious. And I came eating with publicans and sinners, and they didn't like me" (11:16–19, my paraphrase). But the worst of it was that they wouldn't repent.

THE MEASURE OF YOUR JUDGMENT AT THE LAST DAY IS NOT HOW MUCH WICKEDNESS YOU'VE DONE, BUT HOW MUCH LIGHT YOU HAVE REJECTED.

My friend at Orlando First Baptist Church, where they're doing such a tremendous job these days, got me into the pastor's conference in Los Angeles two years ago to speak to the entire congregation of preachers, quite an army of them. And, I said the same thing I had said seventeen years before: The church must first repent. But you don't get many amens on that. They gave me standing ovation, but I wonder how many went home and preached on repentance.

There are too many church members living as though you don't dare preach on repentance too strongly, because the head deacon might take offense and things wouldn't be as pleasant. "But do you mean that Sodom and Gomorrah will fare better on the Day of Judgment than nice Capernaum?" That's what it says.

The measure of your judgment at the last day is not going to be in proportion to how many bad things you've done. I used to think God has the bad things over here and the good things over here; whichever outweighed the other that would determine it. Oh, no—it's not how much wickedness you've done, but how much light you have rejected.

Now, that puts the shoe on another foot. John says, "And this is the condemnation, that light is come into the world, and men loved darkness rather than light, because their deeds were evil." (John 3:19). Ruth Graham said, "If God doesn't judge America, He'll have to apologize to Sodom and Gomorrah."

Jesus said, "For wheresoever the carcase is, there will the eagles be gathered" (Matt. 24:28). Eagles don't feed on carrion, but vultures do—or as we call them in the country, buzzards. At the rate of the rottenness of our society today, this is going to be the biggest buzzard roost of any nation. I wish I knew some sterner way to put it, that might wake somebody up to think it over and do something about it. These people in Capernaum were nice folks, moral people; they wouldn't hurt Jesus for anything, but they just took Him for granted.

Can We Become Too Familiar with Jesus?

Alexander McLaren and his old books are out of style. I don't see them in active use in a lot of preachers' studies anymore. (One said to me, "He's so dry." I said, "Yeah, I used to think that, but I discovered it was Havner who was dry.") McLaren once stood before his nice congregation in England and said to them, "Familiarity with Jesus Christ can be our greatest peril."

That's a fearful way to say it. But you can get so used to it. McLaren said, "I've been standing here for years and you've been sitting there, and I wonder sometimes what you think about what I'm saying. And you have become habituated to what I've told you."

McLaren's words had become like water on a duck's back; it just ran off. He also told his congregation, "You can live so close and so long beside Niagara that you don't hear the water anymore."

Gypsy Smith was asked, "How can you be so fresh and vibrant at your age?" He said, "I've never lost the wonder." Jesus told us about children, told us about the childish, and told us about the childlike. And a revival is when childish church members become childlike and turn to the Lord.

Jesus used a child. I don't know what he'd do today now that the kids are becoming expert at all this new paraphernalia. They'll make us look like a bunch of fuddy-duddies if we can't keep up with it. I believe they ought to be playing hopscotch in the backyard.

One of our magazines came out recently with this line, "What has happened to the magic of childhood?" It isn't there anymore. And, there's some connection there between that and what I'm saying here. Children in the marketplace, playing church, Sunday morning "churchanity" instead of seven days in the week Christ-ianity.

> *"You've told us tonight that God so loved us that if we'll trust His Son we can live forever. How can we sleep when that's true?"*

I think of that Korean missionary who preached to the folks and said, "Now, you're free to go home," and they wouldn't go. He said, "You must get your rest. The meeting is over." One of them stood up and said, "We can't sleep. You've told us tonight that God so loved us that if we'll trust His Son we can live forever. How can we sleep when that's true?"

My soul, we go to sleep listening to it in America—that's no problem at all! That's how we got into this condition. So we must watch it, friends, and I dare to warn you. We need to get back to some straightforward and hard preaching out of this old book.

Listen to Isaiah 1:11–12:

> To what purpose is the multitude of your sacrifices unto me? saith the Lord: I am full of the burnt offerings of rams and the fat of fed beasts; and I delight not in the blood of bullocks, or of lambs, or of the goats. When ye come to appear before me, who hath required this at your hand, to tread my courts?

And then he even hit their tithing and gifts: "Bring no more vain ablations; incense is an abomination unto me . . . even the solemn meeting" (Isa.1:13)—they were so proud of that solemn meeting.

A Warning from the Prophet Amos

Amos has always been my favorite preacher. He was a country preacher, for one thing. And when he went up to preach at Bethel, he had not been invited by the ministerial committee. They invited him to leave, but not to preach.

> Come to Bethel, and transgress; at Gilgal multiply transgression; and bring your sacrifices every morning, and your tithes after three years: And offer a sacrifice of thanksgiving with leaven, and proclaim and publish the free offerings: for this liketh you, O ye children of Israel, saith the Lord God. (Amos 4:4–5)

You may say, "Those old preachers were pretty rough." Well, listen to this from the lips of Jesus Himself: "This people draweth nigh unto me with their mouth, and honoureth me with their lips; but their heart is far from me," (Matt. 15:8).

Jesus said, "When I come back, it'll be like it was in the days of Lot." Well, how was it? Eating and drinking, buying and selling, planting and giving. You may ask, what's wrong with that? Nothing, except God wasn't in it. They weren't living lives according to the will of God.

I know a man who raises hogs, and there's nothing wrong with raising hogs, but I'd hate for hogs to keep me out of heaven, and that's what he's doing. It's a respectable profession, but he has no use for God. It's honorable to make a living, yes. Sometimes, I find church members that need to be jostled severely in this area of their lives.

I was preaching some years ago in a church in Waco, Texas, right next to Baylor University. On Wednesday night, we went over to the Better Religious House. At their invitation, we had the church folks there, we had the students, had the big Baylor choir behind me. And I preached to that crowd the message you are listening to right now.

During the invitation I asked them to sing something not too familiar these days: "The Way of The Cross Leads Home." There are four verses, but I'm only interested in two of them. We'd all vote unanimously for the first verse, that says there is no other way but the way of the cross—that's fine.

But if you want a chill to come over the meeting, try to get people to honestly sing the last verse:

> Then I bid farewell to the way of the world
> to walk in it nevermore.[2]

It's that verse I want you to pay attention to. If we can, with the help of God, separate ourselves from the "ways of the world," we'll never get used to the dark—sin. And we'll never get used to the light—the holy things of God.

And Elisha sent a messenger unto him [Naaman], saying, Go and wash in Jordan seven times.

Second Kings 5:10

When he [Jesus] had thus spoken, he spat on the ground, and made clay of the spittle, and he anointed the eyes of the blind man with the clay, and said unto thim, Go, wash in the pool of Siloam.

John 9:6–7

And the angel of the Lord spake unto Philip, saying, Arise and go toward the south unto the way that goeth down from Jerusalem unto Gaza, which is desert.

Acts 8:26

4

Don't Miss Your Miracle

NAAMAN WAS A captain in the Syrian army. He was a good man militarily and in good favor with King Benadad. I'm sure his chest must have been covered with medals and decorations and stars, but he was a leper. And, when he took off his uniform at night and looked at that decaying body, all the glory of the military departed. There was not a slave in Syria who would have exchanged skins with him.

But there was a sweet little captive girl in his home who knew about his predicament and said, "Oh, if he could only get to the great prophet, he would be healed." And she had such influence in her community that they took her up on it.

They arranged for the reservation of various materials. They got a caravan together, an entourage of money and gifts of different things and took off. And when they arrived at the home of Elisha, this country preacher, he didn't even come to the door. He just sent word, "Go, wash in the Jordan seven times."

Naaman didn't like the way Elisha acted and said, "Who does he think he is? Who does he think I am? The Jordan is nothing but a muddy creek. We've got good rivers up in Syria."

Naaman's servants said, "Well now, if Elisha had asked you to do some big things, you would have done them." So he reluctantly followed Elisha's request.

God had told Naaman to dip himself in the Jordan seven times. So, Naaman went and, ridiculous as he felt, he got in the water and down and up, down and up, one, two, three, four, five, six. Every time he came up, he looked just like he did the last time. But God said seven.

Obedience Brings the Miracle

When God says dip seven times, he doesn't mean just six. And, many a person has missed their blessing because they stopped short of complete obedience to God. When Naaman came up out of the water that last time, his skin was like the flesh of a little child. That's the way God works.

Consider also the blind man going to the pool of Siloam—remember he's still blind—finding his way down the street with mud all over his face. And, folks who knew him said, "Well, what is he up to now? What is he trying to do?"

I sometimes go out to Cannon Beach, Oregon, to a wonderful conference they have out there. It was started by the son of John McNeill, a great Scottish preacher who was a contemporary of D.L. Moody. He was quite a preacher, a Scotsman of real ability and a great sense of humor.

He told me that at one time, he and the church were not getting along with each other. He disappeared for a whole week. Nobody knew where he went. The next Sunday, he showed up in the pulpit, got up and made this simple announcement: "God and John McNeill have come to an understanding. You keep your hands off John McNeill." I think that took care of their problem. Obedience brought the blessing. McNeill delivered the message he felt God had given him.

Bruce Dunne, a great Presbyterian preacher in Peoria, said before he got saved, he was just plain old-fashioned stubborn. He said, "You don't have to publicly walk down an aisle to get saved. I'll get saved in my own way." But walking down the aisle wasn't Dunne's problem. Stubbornness was his problem.

Dunne said, "I got under such conviction one day that I said, "Lord, if I ever make it to church, I'll be willing to turn somersaults down that aisle to get saved." So, God saved him because he got over his stubbornness.

Samuel said to Saul, "Stubbornness is as iniquity and idolatry" (1 Sam. 15:23). We don't think stubbornness is so bad, and we often excuse it. The Bible says stubbornness is bad. So, the greatest tragedy that I know of is the tragedy of the miracles that didn't happen that could have.

Philip was called out of a great revival to go down a long, dusty desert road. There was a eunuch at one end of the road and an evangelist at the other end of the road (see Acts 8:26–39). And, there wouldn't have been any miracle if somebody hadn't obeyed God and gone down the road as directed.

In First Kings 13 we find the only prophet of note in the Bible, whose name we do not know—the unnamed prophet who missed his miracle. God said, "I want you to go and tend to some business for me and do some reproving. But, don't eat with the people you meet. Don't get sociable. And, you take a different road back home."

He started off all right. And the king got under conviction, tried to lay hands on him, and was stricken with leprosy and had to pray for help.

There was an old retired backslidden preacher living out in the country somewhere around there, and his boys came home and said, "Man, you ought to have been downtown this morning. A revival really started. Even the king got under conviction." The preacher had been out of the will of God a long time, but that news of revival stirred up better memories and he said, "Well, go get him; have him come here and eat."

When the prophets' servants invited the man of God to a meal he said, "I'm not supposed to eat with anyone." And then, the old backslider told the man of God that he too was a prophet, and that God wanted him to come and eat at his house. But he was lying! With that statement, the man of God from Bethel went to eat at the home of the prophet with no name—and tragically lost his life as a result.

It's a tragic thing to miss your miracle.

You know, you've got to watch these people that know God's will for your life more than you do. They'll get you in more trouble than anybody else I know. If God wants you to do something, He'll tell you.

Alexander Whyte, in his incomparable style, said that when the two prophets sat down, there was a sense of awe at first. The old prophet was in the presence of reality again. And, as the two started cracking jokes and getting sociable, the prophet of God became just another prophet. And so, Alexander Whyte goes into some needed advice for preachers today about getting sociable too soon after the sermon.

Sometimes the blessing of what was preached disappears in the Sunday dinner. Too often, preachers try to become the life of the party and they often wonder why their message and their role as a spiritual leader isn't taken seriously. Let the tragedy of the disobedient prophet be a warning to all of us. It's a tragic thing to miss your miracle.

I was at Moody's Founder's Week two years ago and, of course, the wonderful Gray Auditorium was filled, as it always is for that occasion. Of course, there were many students at the meeting, but there were also middle-aged and older people. I got my heart set on them somehow that night, and I didn't say much to the students. I said to the old folks, "I have a feeling tonight there are ladies listening to me whom God once called to be a missionary, but you didn't go. And, there may be some men here whom God called to be preachers, but they never preached." And I went down that line, and when the time came for a show of hands, I was amazed at their sincere response.

My daddy was called to preach and never preached. He was a good man. He had one brother who was a Baptist preacher and one a Methodist preacher. It was pretty hard to get an education in those days. Dad had a family in those days, and he didn't have much money, and he kept putting off going into the ministry. But, for the rest of his days, he was not happy. He realized he'd missed the main thing.

When I started preaching, he was so happy. But, he didn't make a preacher out of me. I never knew the day I didn't feel called to be a preacher. But my father did the next best thing. He was as faithful as he could be at Old Corinth Baptist Church. In the winter he would be at the church early in the morning and make a fire in that old stove and taught a Bible class and won people to Jesus Christ in that community.

There was a young fellow who came to know the Lord because of my dad's blunt way of speaking to him. My father tried to witness to him. He said, "Oh, Mr. Havner, I'm a young man. What are you talking about? I've got lots of time." Dad couldn't stand that kind of talk. He said, "You remind me of a fellow in the Bible that God called a fool."

I wouldn't put that in books on soul winning. I don't think that's the correct approach, in general. But it worked. Two weeks later, the young man walked down the aisle. The pastor asked the young man, "What brings you here?" And he said in substance, "I don't want to be that man God called a fool in the Bible. I don't want to be like that. I've got time, and I'm using it to come to Jesus."

Father was faithful to the very last, because I leaned over him as he changed worlds, and the last thing I heard him try to sing was, "Jesus paid it all, and all to Him I owe."

There was a time in my ministry when I was about to miss God's blessing. And, then I met that well-known, Bible-preaching evangelist, R.A. Torrey, on a train. And, he asked me, "What are you doing?" I tried to think of something I was doing right fast, and I couldn't think of a thing in the world.

He said, "Young man, make up your mind on one thing and stay with it." He didn't want me to be like a broom with straws pointing in all directions, but like a sword with one point. This one thing I do.

I've gone to Montrose many a time where he lies buried, climbed that hill and stood at that grave and thanked God for that preacher. He looked like an old, rugged, bearded prophet. He didn't play games at all. Dr. Torrey's exhortation helped me to refocus my preaching ministry on the absolute truth of God's Word.

Perhaps you heard the voice of God years ago, and you've not been obedient to God's call. It may be too late for some things. You may not be able to go to China or Africa now as a missionary. But I want to bear news to you that just as when Jesus fed the multitude, and a multitude it was, they had twelve basketsful left over, not crumbs, but what hadn't been used in the first place.

Everybody has a little left over. You may not have much time left, but be determined to be obedient to God with the time you do have left. Get on your knees and say to God, "I want you to be the 'Lord of the leftovers' of my life." No telling what God can do with some older folks. I'm seeing more forty-year-olds go into the ministry than I've seen in all my life. Something is working on these fellows that missed it the first time, and now they're going. It's late, but they're doing better than some that go half-heartedly to school all those years and don't learn much anyhow. Who knows what miracle might come out of the decision you make right now?

I wonder sometimes what Jesus would have done with some of the fellows who missed their miracle. How about the rich young ruler? He had manners and morals and money—and that's a pretty good combination, if you know how to use it. What did God want to do with the rich young ruler? Nobody will ever know. You just can't tell.

I get so tired of these folks who say the day of miracles is past. Wherever did you get that idea in your head? What is a miracle? Webster has a pretty good definition: "An event that appears unexplainable by the laws of nature but is held to be of supernatural origin or an act of God." That's pretty good, for a dictionary. And, that's what it is.

Please remember that God is not contra-natural. He doesn't break His own laws. He's supernatural when it suits His purpose. Jesus Christ was a miracle when He came down here. He died a miracle death and had a miracle resurrection and went to heaven miraculously and coming back is a miracle all the way through. And, if you live for Him, it's a miracle life.

Galatians 2:20 says, "I am crucified with Christ: nevertheless I live; yet not I, but Christ liveth in me: and the life which I now live in the flesh I live by the faith of the Son of God, who loved me, and gave himself for me."

We call Jesus Savior—most folks do, if they claim to be Christians. Not many get around to making him Lord, and almost none ever get to the other word; He is our life. The life you now live in the flesh, this time in the sense not of the old nature, but the body. Why you live it is because there's somebody else living it within you, if you're a Christian. But the trouble today is the church can't get to the goal for stumbling over its own team.

We furnish our own greatest interference in the church today. It's our crowd that's causing more trouble than anybody else, because they're not living the Christian life. We need a miracle in the church. The Pentecost was a miracle. The church is a miracle. Christian life is a miracle.

We talk about doing what comes naturally. God wants us to do what comes *super*naturally by the grace of God. God has a miracle life for you. To live is not to live like Christ or for Christ, to live is Christ. That's what Paul said it is.

But we never can know
the delights of His love
until all on the altar we lay.
For the favor He shows
and the joy He bestows
are for them who will trust and obey.[1]

I used to ride the trains a lot; I don't like flying, but I love to ride. And there's only one railroad that will get you to heaven, and that's the old T&O—trust and obey.

In the last day, that great day of the feast, Jesus stood and cried, saying, if any man thirst, let him come unto me, and drink. He that believeth on me, as the scripture hath said, out of his belly shall flow rivers of living water. (But this spake he of the Spirit, which they that believe on him should receive: for the Holy Ghost was not yet given; because that Jesus was not yet glorified.)

John 7:37–39

5

If Any Man Thirst

JESUS WAS AT the feast of tabernacles. It was all the feasts, you might say, rolled into one. It was the big religious day of the year for the people where our Lord ministered. And they commemorated the deliverance in the wilderness, the water from the rock, and so on. The priest would go to the pool of Siloam, fill a pitcher with water and come back down to the temple followed by the happy throng of people, and he would pour out the water while they sang, "Therefore with joy shall ye draw water out of the wells of salvation" (Isa. 12:3).

It was such a hilarious occasion; it was said whoever has not witnessed it has never seen rejoicing at all.

Of course, all this singing was religious and all of it in one way or the other revolved around the expected and hoped-for Messiah. But on this occasion, *the Messiah was there*, though not many people paid any attention to Him.

A strange picture it must have made. There Jesus stood, and as He watched this demonstration, He was impressed only by the futility of the whole business. Why didn't He say, "Oh, this is grand to see all this religious celebration. I'm so glad to be with you"?

Jesus knew a lot of it was pious humbug, because they all went home after it was over with the same old headaches and the same old heartaches, the same old doubts and fears. And it looked like a great success, the talk of the year. "Are you going up to the feast of tabernacles?"

Jesus stood and cried out loud. That wasn't His way of speaking, because the Bible said it wasn't His usual style. "He shall not strive nor cry; neither shall any man hear his voice in the streets" (Matt. 12:19). But this time, he raised His voice and cried out, "If anybody here is thirsty" (water was their main interest at that moment) "let him come to me."

He stands in this lost world, a world dying of soul starvation, in the midst of all its celebrations and heart thirsts, and hungering for a real spiritual sustenance.

Scientifically Advanced, But Still Thirsty

We're smart; scientifically, we're the smartest we've ever been. Two weeks ago, I sat at the table with a rather shy gentleman. His wife came up and asked, "May we sit with you?" I said yes. It took me half an hour after that to find out who they were and what it was all about. He was one of the first three men who went to the moon.

Well, you don't meet celebrities like that every day of the week! I tried to get this shy gentleman to tell me what the most fascinating moment of that historical trip to the moon was.

His short reply was, "When I stood there and watched the old earth receding, getting further and further away and it wasn't any bigger than a dime, and every living being in existence was on it. There you stand and see it; that little ball of earth drifting away from you. You begin wondering if you'll ever get back home."

But he also said he was impressed with the greatness of the almighty God as never before. I learned he and his wife were devoted to the Lord in a very deep and real way.

When America first sent men to the moon, I was in Jacksonville, Florida. I saw them lift off as I watched TV from my motel room. At the same time, I could look out the window into a park that I didn't dare to walk in alone for fear I'd be clobbered and robbed. Smart enough to walk on the moon but not safe enough to walk in the park—that's America.

As a boy, we had our revival at Old Corinth Baptist Church, in Vale, NC, between Hickory and Shelby. We never thought about locking up the house when we went to church. Nobody was going to bother it. You don't feel that way about it now.

I travel all over the country and live in motels. I was in one the other day where they had the telephone screwed to the table. They're taking no chances. I heard of a woman who said, "What in the world are we coming to? Somebody broke in my house and stole all my Holiday Inn towels."

I read an article somebody wrote about the World's Fair. They said the World's Fair was a demonstration of the advances of science and their application through industry, to create a larger life for all mankind. The article went on to say we could see the forward movements of science and their application through industry, but we looked in vain for the larger life for all mankind.

You see, Ephesus has left its first love. Pergamum, with Thyatira, has gone all out for Balaam and Jezebel. Sardis, the living faith of the dead, has become the dead faith of the living. Laodicea was neither hot nor cold, but lukewarm. We ought to remember that Jesus said he prefers a cold church to a warm one. “I would thou wert cold or hot” (Rev. 3:15). That’s what zealous means, “not lukewarm.”

Sometimes, in the restaurant when the waitress comes up and says, “May I warm up your coffee?” I say to her, “No, pour this out and let’s start over. I don’t want any Laodicean coffee.” She probably doesn’t know what Laodicean coffee is, but I expect you do!

The Lord doesn’t like that kind of church. He said, “You make me sick.” It isn’t an elegant phrase that he uses—“I will spue thee out of my mouth” (3:16). You know what that is. It’s churches that are neither cold nor hot, neither good nor bad, just so-so. And we have plenty of those types of churches today.

Thirst

“If any man thirst” is the first requirement here, and that indicates desperation. Thirsting is not just casually wanting a drink of water; thirst is getting so desperate for a drink of water it’s all you can think about. And this holy thirst for God is getting to the place where nothing else will satisfy you.

All the way through the Bible, every one of the great heroes of faith were desperate people: Daniel in the lion’s den, the Hebrew children in the fiery furnace, Elijah and Isaiah, Mary, Martha, and Lazarus, the disciples in the storm, Jacob at Jabbok, Moses at the Red Sea, David facing Goliath, the four lepers at the gate of Samaria—and so it goes, every one of them on the spot, desperate.

Jesus made it so simple here: thirsting, coming, drinking, believing, and overflowing. Thirsting and then coming to Him. And then there’s where faith comes in, receive it just like you did for salvation, according to God’s word, according to God's will, according to your need, and according to your faith. God will answer any prayer that's according to those four. You can't miss. Is it according to His word, His will, my need, and my faith? You get those four in a row and you're ready to pray with true confidence.

TO BE FILLED WITH THE HOLY SPIRIT, YOUR LIFE'S PURPOSE MUST BE TO GLORIFY CHRIST.

It says in John 7:39 that the Spirit was not yet given because Jesus was not yet glorified. Of course, that refers to His death and the resurrection and Pentecost. But one reason some Christians aren't filled with the Spirit is because they wouldn't glorify Jesus if they were filled. The purpose of your life must be to glorify Jesus Christ. He's not giving the Holy Spirit just to attract attention.

God, help us keep our church events from becoming like this great crowd at the feast! It was one of the biggest crowds you could get together for a religious meeting, yet it meant nothing. And I get into some meetings today that I don't think mean much.

In some great church gatherings, I watch politicking and self-promotion going on among some of the brethren. They think you must know "key men" to get things accomplished. You don't have to know the key man. All you need to know is the keeper of the keys. He's got all of them right on His belt, and He can open any door that needs opening, if you know Him. An awful lot of politicking goes on in the name of religion today, and I don't think God is pleased with it. It doesn't get us anywhere.

We Need to Get on Fire

I love to hear Dr. E.V. Hill from California preach to us preachers. He once said, "When I get here with all you theologians, I'm glad I majored in agriculture." And then he really went to town, and added, "You Southern Baptists, you've got a lot of stuff, if you could just get it on fire."

Well, that's right. We've got a lot of stuff, but it's not on fire, and it needs to get on fire. And Methodists, Presbyterians, and whatever, you've got stuff, too, but it needs to catch on fire.

I don't mean we shouldn't have hilarious meetings of the right kind. There are at least three places in the Bible where they had a musical, hilarious time. When David danced before the ark, that wife he'd married was anything but joyous. She said, "You certainly were a pretty sight out there bouncing around over the flesh." And that's what the world always says when a Christian gets happy.

And then, you remember the time when Jesus cleansed the temple, and little children were singing Hosanna and waving palm branches? And guess who didn't like that? The religious people. "These kids are making too much racket here."

I've heard that in church. You can do it, of course, the wrong way. I know that. But here the folks who read the Bible, prayed in public, were tithers, tried to win others, lived moral lives—and went to hell. That was the Sadducees, the religious element of His day.

It tells in that same 7th chapter of John they started talking about Jesus. Some said, "Well, He's the Messiah." Some said, "No, I don't think so. He didn't come from the right part of the country." And there was a division among the people. Some would have taken Him, but no man laid hands on Him.

And the officers came along and the Jewish leaders asked, "Haven't you brought Him?" The officers said, "Never a man spoke like Him." And then the Pharisees answered, "Are you also deceived? Have any of the rulers believed on Him? But these people, they don't know anything." Then Nicodemus spoke up and said, "Well, let's give Him a fair trial."

All kinds of ideas about Jesus, we still have them. There's talk like that to this day.

Have you noticed the sad way this chapter ends? But they said, "Why, He's from the wrong place. Search and find out, for out of Gallilee riseth no prophet." And every man went to his own house.

And they're still doing it today—walking away from Jesus, arguing about Him. Is He the one? He doesn't fit this picture; He doesn't fit that picture.

But the first verse of the next chapter is a sad chapter: "Jesus went out alone to the Mount of Olives." He's still doing it in many a situation. It's only the thirsty who are invited here.

Have you ever thirsted, desperately desired what you lack, in this matter of being filled with the Holy Spirit? Jesus has made it very simple. And I thank God that he said, "come." He is always inviting you and me to come to Him. Thirst, come, drink, receive; that's what that means. James says, "If any of you lack wisdom, let him ask of God, that giveth to all men liberally, and upbraideth not; and it shall be given him" (James 1:5).

I believe if you mean business with God and everything is right between you and God and others, you've got a right to get down on your knees and ask God for what you need and get up and believe you got it. That's what He says.

Dr. R.A. Torrey said that Mark 11:24 worried him: "What things soever ye desire, when ye pray, believe that ye receive them, and ye shall have them." Believe that you've got it, and you'll get it. He said the grammar didn't come out right. He had to get to the place where he said, "Forget the grammar; I'm going to go ahead and believe it anyhow." We have to reach that place. We need wisdom as never before and there's only one way to get it.

The children of Issachar, in the Old Testament, had understanding of the times to know what Israel ought to do. If there's anything church people need today, it's understanding, a knowledge of the times!

It's an understanding of the times that produced the knowledge, not a knowledge that produced understanding. We get it backwards. We read up a lot on the times and don't know any more than we did. Understanding the times in the light of God's Word and the light of prayer, and then we know what the application is, what God's people ought to do. That's the way. But we must come in faith believing.

Do you ever wonder why your life is so barren of overflowing blessing? You know, we used to have an old song by James Brockman entitled "I'm Forever Blowing Bubbles." I said, "Lord, I don't want to be a bubble blower; I want to be a blessing bringer."

Now, you can do that. I don't care what you do for a living. Some of the greatest "blessing bringers" in this world are the commonest, plainest people at some ordinary job. Preachers have got too much theology sometimes for all that. Some folks don't know any better than to be usable in the hands of almighty God. Come to Jesus just like a little child.

The sweetest illustration I've heard is simply about faith. It was dry weather, and the crops were in danger, and the church put on a prayer meeting. Someone suggested, "Let's meet and pray for rain."

There was quite a group assembled, and only one little girl brought a little bitty umbrella. And a lady said, "Honey, why are you bringing that umbrella? There's not a cloud in the sky."

She said, "We're going to pray for rain. If God sends rain, we'll need umbrellas."

Now, that's faith, that's simple faith. I want to be more like that. "What things soever ye desire, when ye pray, believe that ye receive them, and ye shall have them" (Mark 11:24).

It's not sermons we need, it's doing something about the sermons we've already heard. If your life is barren, if you're not overflowing with a blessing to others, come and drink and keep on drinking, and the blessing will follow. Don't watch for the blessing; let God keep the books. Go to Jesus and mean business, and you'll see things begin to happen.

May each of us give to God a similar prayer that says, "Lord, if I've got a thirst, create in my soul a burning thirst for God's best. Help me to get to Jesus to drink, to believe, and to overflow."

Now Peter and John went up together into the temple at the hour of prayer, being the ninth hour. And a certain man lame from his mother's womb was carried, whom they laid daily at the gate of the temple which is called Beautiful, to ask alms of them that entered into the temple; who seeing Peter and John about to go into the temple asked an alms. And Peter, fastening his eyes upon him with John, said, Look on us. And he gave heed unto them, expecting to receive something of them. Then Peter said, Silver and gold have I none; but such as I have give I thee: In the name of Jesus Christ of Nazareth rise up and walk. And he took him by the right hand, and lifted him up: and immediately his feet and anklebones received strength. And he leaping up stood, and walked, and entered with them into the temple, walking, and leaping, and praising God. . . . For the man was above forty years old, on whom this miracle of healing was shewed.

Acts 3:1–8; 4:22

6

Miracles after Forty

THE CRIPPLED MAN in Acts the third chapter, who lay at the gate of the Temple, began his day as usual, begging. He probably thought it would be another humdrum day, just like any other.

But according to our text it was anything but an ordinary day—it was a miraculous day. On this day, Peter and John showed up, and the power of God came down. The man, who had never walked, leaped and changed from monotony to miracle and from sorrow to shouting.

In this account you have first tribulation, then transformation, then testimony. We read in 4:14 that, when accusation was made against Peter and John, they beheld the man which was healed standing with them, and could say nothing against him. That was the unanswerable argument. There he stood, a healed man.

Notice the postscript found in 4:22: "For the man was above forty years old, on whom this miracle of healing was shewed." There is more than a passing significance attached to this verse.

Why would the Holy Spirit go to the trouble to tell us the man was over forty years of age? Well, for one reason, when anything miraculous happens to anybody over forty, it's worth an extra verse. Most people get in a rut by age forty, and rusted in the groove. They tell us "life begins at forty," and it did for this poor crippled man, but a great many other things can happen to us at forty. Sometimes, rigor mortis sets in about this time.

A Focus on Youth

A great deal of attention is given to the youth of our day. But I'm concerned tonight with some of the rest of us. We preachers never hesitate to preach to young people when there are plenty of older people in the congregation. Why should we hesitate to preach to older people if there are young people in the congregation? All young people need is a little time and they will be in the same category. We are in great and drastic need today of something miraculous happening to the forty-year-old and older class.

The first half of our lives we are romantic and the second half we are rheumatic. (Of course, I've known some rheumatics who become romantic, and lost their rheumatism even after forty!) But life does not need to flatten out after forty.

We have unfortunately taken the attitude, "Let the young people go forward; we have all we expect to have from the Lord; we've arrived; we don't intend to take in much more spiritual territory." The biggest problem I'm up against today in meetings in churches over the land is that solid block of folks forty years old and older who just sit there, set in their ways, looking for young people to make all the dedications.

Thank God for the young people! I don't know what would happen to some of our services if they didn't summon enough energy by the grace of God to make a move. But unless something happens to this older generation, we are not going to have revival. When fresh cement is poured, you can make the slightest imprint upon it, and it will remain through the years; but let it harden, and an elephant can walk across it and make no impression at all.

The Bible speaks of those who are set in their ways and have not been emptied from vessel to vessel. People get into that condition, like a jar of milk that has turned to curds or vinegar with a crust on top of it. Sometimes we get in that condition and we need to be emptied from vessel to vessel. And that's what revival is.

THE HARDEST PART OF THE JOURNEY OF LIFE IS THE MIDDLE MILE.

Revival is the churning up of the church of God and emptying from vessel to vessel. All one needs to do is to check on how many have been saved before they were fifteen, and how many fifteen to twenty-five, and then on up, and you would instantly see what I mean. The biggest problem in this life on earth is the middle mile. It's the hardest part of the journey. There's a certain exhilaration at the beginning and there's a certain thrill at the close, but it's the middle mile that tests the traveler.

I grew up in red dirt country, and I used to have to hoe corn and cotton. We would start out early in the morning, and at the end of the day I always stuck the hoe up at the end of a corn row, so I'd know where to resume my hoeing the next morning. There was no other way of telling which row had been hoed and which hadn't been hoed.

In the morning, although I didn't care particularly for hoeing corn, I would start out with a youthful zest, and in the evening, when the day's work was done and we started back up that long, old hill to the house on top of the ridge, I was weary physically, but there was still a certain exhilaration about the day's work.

But ah, the middle of the day, after we had our noon meal and had to go back to that salt mine! That tested me. I didn't need an expositor to explain what "the burden and heat of the day" (Matt. 20:12) meant. I understood that full well.

The Challenge of Middle Age

Youth and old age have their delights. But when the sunrise glow has disappeared and the sunset has not yet filled the west, that is the test. My heart goes out to older people. They're the backbone of the church. They carry the financial burden. If they're not as starry-eyed as they once were, it's because they've learned some things from experience. And I want to rouse them as I go about my preaching ministry from their midday nap, as it were.

Somebody has said youth has fire without light and age has light without fire. And we need the proper combination of both so we may be what John the Baptist was, a burning and a shining light. He had both. We shouldn't leave all the fire to youth, and we shouldn't leave all the light to age but combining them, let them shine together to the glory of God.

Revival must come to all ages. Do you remember the plea Joel made? The only verse out of Joel that most people know is the one Peter quoted on the day of Pentecost. But there are some terrific things in this little book. Joel was a revivalist, and he called in Joel 2:16–17,

> Gather the people, sanctify the congregation, assemble the elders, gather the children and those that suck the breasts: let the bridegroom go forth of his chamber and the bride out of her closet. Let the priests, the ministers of the LORD, weep between the porch and the altar and let them say, Spare thy people, O LORD, and give not thine heritage to reproach, that the heathen should rule over them: wherefore should they say among the people, Where is their God?

That, I submit to you, was *not* a youth revival.

Families used to sit together at church. That, of course, is all a thing of the past. And some of the elderly people haven't walked down a church aisle since they were in their teens. We need a return to this in this day of the split churches and split personalities and split atoms; even the family splits before it ever gets to church. Some never go, and others do nothing about the opportunity after they arrive. But God's program is not limited to any age group whatsoever.

Rehoboam ruined his kingdom and wrecked his career because he listened to the rash advice of youth and ignored the sober counsel of age. We are in danger of doing that, too. The churches want pastors so young nowadays that a preacher is almost outmoded at forty-five years of age!

It's time for preaching on some such text as "Let not him that girdeth on his harness boast himself as he that putteth it off" (1 Kings 20:11). There's no special brand of Christianity for young people. I get a little amused today at these youth churches and youth gospels and youth everything else. Why, you'd think young people had just been invented. We've had them ever since I can remember.

All that youth need to do is what they've always done. They all sin, and they need to repent, and they need to confess their sins and present their bodies as living sacrifices and put on the Lord Jesus and make not provision for the flesh just like everybody else. There isn't any peculiar brand of Christianity for young people.

We need a family revival in the church of God today. And we need particularly to be guarded against what Psalm 91:6 calls "the destruction that wasteth at noonday."

There are many reasons older people ought to be the first ones to go to the mourner's bench. Theirs is the responsibility of example, for one thing. We've been on the road longer. We ought to be the best Christians in the entire outfit. But sometimes brand-new Christians are better witnesses. Sometimes, the best soul winner is the fellow just fresh out of sin and all aglow with his new experience.

I've often said the happiest fellow in the world is a brand-new Christian—before he's met too many Bible scholars, doesn't know any better than to believe it just like it reads, and is full of zeal and enthusiasm. And then, ours is the responsibility of the home, the foundation of our national life. As goes the home, so goes the nation. And the older people are the head and the heart of the home.

We older folks are to show youth how to be responsible with money. Of course, young people have more money than they used to have, but older people generally have the larger supply of it, and theirs is the responsibility to use it wisely.

We elders are also to be responsible with our time, because we don't have much left. When you don't have much money, you must spend it very carefully. And when time is running out on you, you need to be extra careful about being a good steward with what years or maybe months are left to you. I used to say I would do this or that when I got to be twenty, or thirty, or forty, and so on, and now I realize I haven't many more decades, if any, to count on.

The less we have, the more carefully we ought to spend it, buying up its opportunities because the days are evil.

I also feel a responsibility now, coming with a new lease on life and a new extension of time granted me by the direct intervention of God in response to the prayers of His people.

Some time ago, I passed through a night when I was very ill and closer to heaven than earth. And the head nurse on that floor was a fine Christian who had worked all day, and she volunteered to sit up all night with me.

Many a time through the night, I looked out of that oxygen tent, and there she was. When she wasn't watching me, she was praying. And along about the middle of the night, I said, "Let's claim the promise." I didn't have enough breath to say much. But she took my hand, and we claimed the promise, "That if two of you shall agree on earth as touching any thing that they shall ask, it shall be done" (Matt. 18:19).

You don't have to come through a hospital experience, of course, to have a new lease on life. Sometimes, God grants it in other ways. I think of those lines that Amy Carmichael used to quote:

> What though I live with the winners
> Or perish with those who fall?
> Only the cowards are sinners
> Fighting the fight is all.
> Strong is my foe—he advances!
> Snapt is my blade, O Lord!
> See the proud banners and lances!
> Oh, spare me this stub of a sword![1]

Some of us are battling out the rest of our days with only the stub of a sword. But you can do a good job for God with the stub of a sword. Some haven't yet begun to live for God, and they only have a stub of a sword left. Why don't you turn that over to the Lord? Yes, thank God, He can give you a brand-new sword of the Spirit with which to spend your declining years. It's a solemn and a serious responsibility.

Remember Paul's wish that he might finish his course with joy. You're never safe till the last step. If you're in Christ Jesus, yes, you're safe for time and eternity. But as far as your witness and your testimony and the usefulness of your life, you're never safe till you get clear across.

So many have started out gloriously and they've run well. And then within sight of the goal, they have finished miserably. What a fool a man can be after forty or fifty!

Moses did pretty well the first forty, and it was later in life that he made his big blunder. David, as a shepherd boy on the hills of Bethlehem, did right well; but David, a king in a palace, fell miserably.

Gideon, in the early chapters, was a noble warrior for the Lord, but it was after forty, in the later chapters, that he slipped. King Asa walked close to the Lord in the early part of his life—then came to that day when he turned away from the Lord and turned to man, and the last chapter wasn't so good.

Paul said, "I have fought a good fight, I have finished my course, I have kept the faith" (2 Tim. 4:7). No wonder he kept his body under subjection. And well he might have prayed the prayer of the psalmist, "Now also when I am old and gray-headed, O God, forsake me not until I have showed Thy strength unto this generation and Thy power to everyone that is to come" (Ps.71:18).

I think it was Bishop John Taylor Smith who prayed, "God, keep me from being a wicked old man." It's amazing how one can stumble in the last round of this fight. There's a danger of resting on the oars. We may have mounted up with wings as eagles in youth; we may have run well in middle age; and then we fail to walk and not faint (see Isa. 40:31).

The Prevailing Sin of Middle Age

One of my friends in the North, speaking of a great preacher whose name I will not mention, said, "There was a time in my life when he was my greatest inspiration. And then there came a time when he was my greatest warning." Isn't that a tragedy, to start out an inspiration and become a warning sign?

The sin of middle age is complacency, smugness, lukewarmness, and leaving one's first love—and getting used to it. It need not be so, because the last years can be the best. I heard of two preachers who were talking on Monday, and one said to the other, "I preached to older people yesterday, and I'll venture you can't guess what my text was."

The other said, "'At evening time, it shall be light' (Zech. 14:7)?"

"No."

"'The hoary head is a crown of glory' (Prov. 16:31)?"

"No."

"Well, I give up," he said, "what was it"?

He said, "I preached about the parable of the laborers in the vineyard where the Lord said to the eleventh-hour crowd, 'Go ye also into the vineyard' (Matt.20:7)." Nobody is exempt!

Look at the last verse of this chapter's text: "For the man was above forty years old, on whom this miracle of healing was shewed" (Acts 4:22).

Nobody looks much for miracles after forty. They don't look for miracles at any age these days. Scoffers say, "All things continue as they were; everything runs the natural course. There aren't any miracles. God doesn't break through."

And yet magazines and books are filled with recipes of success and happiness after middle age—how to stay young and look pretty and be happy. Millions have tried these recipes, but with little success. And all because we want a miracle. We'd love to have all kinds of miracles, but we secure so few of them.

Let's Not Question God

You remember what Gideon said? The land was under the thumb of a foreign power, and here was old Gideon trying to beat out a little grain—and all of a sudden, an angel appeared! The appearance of an angel is a miracle—something that doesn't happen every day of the week. But Gideon is so down in the dumps he says, "If the LORD be with us, why then is all this befallen us? and where be all his miracles which our fathers told us of?" (Judges 6:13).

There are people today asking that, and yet we shouldn't do it, because every Sunday morning in church you're right in the middle of a miracle. When you hold the Word of God in your hand, that's a miracle. If you've been born again, that's a miracle. How foolish to sit in a gathering and say, "Where are the miracles?"

Of course, a lot of church members have not been converted today. They don't know what this miracle means. They are not operating on a miracle basis. Nothing has happened to them that couldn't have happened if the Holy Spirit had gone out of business.

There are some churches operating today that would not know the difference if the Holy Spirit ceased to work. But I thank God miracles are happening. When John the Baptist had the blues in jail and sent a delegation to Jesus, he was asking Jesus such questions as, "Art thou he that should come, or do we look for another?" (Matt. 11:3).

John the Baptist was the last man you'd expect to ask such a question! Why, he'd stood on the banks of the Jordan and proclaimed Jesus was the Messiah as a glorious affirmation. And now it had become an interrogation.

I'm so glad, however, that my Lord didn't bawl him out. The Lord didn't send back a scorching message of reproof and say, "I'm ashamed of you. You ought to know better than that." Not at all. "For he knoweth our frame; he remembereth that we are dust" (Ps. 103:14).

Instead, He sent back this word: "Go and shew John again those things which ye do hear and see: The blind receive their sight and the lame walk, the lepers are cleansed, and the deaf hear, the dead are raised up, and the poor have the gospel preached to them. And blessed is he, whosoever shall not be offended in me" (Matt. 11:4–6). He said, "Tell John that I am still in the miracle business!"

Everybody knows the beatitudes in the Sermon on the Mount. But Matthew 11:6 has the one I call the forgotten beatitude: "Blessed is he who is not upset by the way I run my business!" (my paraphrase).

I hear Christians say, "Why in the world isn't he or she being converted? Why aren't things working out the way I thought they would? Lord, do we need to start looking for somebody else?"

The Lord says, "No, I'm doing what I started to do. I began it way back there in Luke, and I'm still carrying on what I began to do and teach. It's the unfinished work. I'm carrying it on. And blessed are you if you don't get upset about it." Can you claim the beatitude of the unfounded?

Expect Miracles Every Day

There are others that after forty settle down after conversion and don't expect another miracle till the resurrection. My friend, you are due several. Better than vitamins, you are due many a day. You ought to live from one miracle to another.

Dr. Ironside used to tell about an old lady that would get up in every testimony meeting and start out, "Forty years ago . . ." and Ironside said, "I just wanted to say, 'Dear sister, whatever happened to you forty years ago, thank the Lord for it, but hasn't anything happened since?'"

I'll thank God for that happy day that fixed our choice on Him, our Savior and our God, but "The path of the just is as the shining light, that shineth more and more unto the perfect day" (Prov. 4:18).

Our Christian life is a miracle—miraculous in its origin, because it's the gift of God; miraculous in its operation, by the grace of God; and miraculous in its objective, to the glory of God. And there ought to be miracles every day. I don't mean handling rattlesnakes without being poisoned, but I mean miracles of guidance and answered prayer and victory and soul winning.

We don't need to keep scrubbing up some old experience that happened way back when. Every day we ought to shine with the presence of God. You *can* have a miracle after forty!

I preached many years ago in a little country church near Davidson, North Carolina. I was entertained that week in the home of a poor farmer—and I mean *poor*. And he was very green—unsophisticated. The poor fellow not only didn't know anything, I don't think he even suspected anything. He was so green, I believe if he hadn't kept moving, he'd have taken root and sprouted!

I stayed in his home, and they put me in a little corner. It wasn't a room; it was just the corner of the house with a kind of a sheet up in front of it to seclude me from the rest of the house. In the morning, I'd have to look out to make sure the coast was clear before I could venture out.

I preached all week and not a soul moved. I never saw such immobile people in all my life. I began to wonder why I ever wasted a week on this crowd. Nobody cared whether they ever heard the call of God or not.

But who do you suppose heard the call of God that week? That dear man over forty! He heard God's call, went back to school, and became a Presbyterian minister. If I went over that community with a fine-toothed comb looking for a prospect, he would have been the last man I would have selected. But I never despair of the grace of God and the power of my heavenly Father to work miracles after forty.

Sometimes we get rather churlish and set in our ways after forty. I think of a godly woman who was married to an unbeliever, and she'd prayed all through the years that he might be saved. He showed no sign of interest in spiritual things. But a revival meeting was held in the community, and he fairly astounded her one evening by saying, "I think I'll go with you to church." And he went. God spoke to him, and he got saved.

The next morning as she was preparing breakfast, he said from the other room, "I want you to come over here and look out the window." And she came, and, although it was a barren, winter landscape with not a leaf on the trees, he said, "Isn't that the prettiest sight you ever saw in all your life?"

He said, "It seems like the very trees want to clap their hands." Well, he had scripture for that: "For ye shall go out with joy, and be led forth with peace: the mountains and the hills shall break forth before you into singing, and all the trees of the field shall clap their hands" (Isa. 55:12). Miracles after forty!

I recall holding a meeting in Altoona, Pennsylvania. One afternoon as we rode home from the service, there was a sweet old man in the back seat of the car. He'd been saved when he was sixty-nine and now he was seventy-eight. He got in at the last chapter. And as we drove along, my friend in the front seat said to him, "Why don't you recite your favorite poem for Brother Havner?"

And with rare diction and with a wealth of feeling that I couldn't possibly equal, this dear soul began to quote those amazing lines of Martha Snell Nicholson:

When I stand at the judgment seat of Christ,
And He shows me His plan for me,
The plan of my life as it might have been
Had He had His way, and I see.
How I blocked Him here and I checked Him there,
And I would not yield my will,

Will there be grief in my Savior's eyes,
Grief, though he loves me still?
He would have made me rich, and I stand there poor,
Stripped of all but His grace
While memory runs like a hunted thing
Down the path I cannot retrace.
Then my desolate heart will well-nigh break
With the tears that I cannot shed;
I shall cover my face with my empty hands,
I shall bow my uncrowned head.
Lord of the years that are left to me,
I give them to Thy hands.
Take me and break me and mold me to
The pattern Thou hast planned.[2]

Well, bless his heart, he got into the kingdom of God at sixty-nine, and he'd had nine years to praise God. Miracles will come well after forty.

I am concerned with dear friends these days who are letting life slip by, and the sands have almost run out and you don't know for sure that you're a child of God or you haven't really yet committed all you are and have to Him. Maybe you're saying, "Well, there's no use; my life is spent. I couldn't be a missionary. There isn't much time left."

My dear friend, you're the one who ought to commit your life to Christ immediately, because you don't have much time left. If you are an elderly person and still haven't yielded your life to the Lord, I encourage you to pray soon and say,

> *I haven't much time left, but God, You have been gracious enough to wait on me all this time; certainly the least that I can do is to make a commitment to You and say, "Dear Lord, I give myself to Thee, it's all that I can do."*

I am come to send fire on the earth; and what will I, if it be already kindled? But, I have a baptism to be baptized with; and how am I straitened till it be accomplished! Suppose ye that I am come to give peace on earth? I tell you, Nay; but rather division: For from henceforth there shall be five in one house divided, three against two and two against three. The father shall be divided against the son, and the son against the father; the mother against the daughter, and the daughter against the mother; the mother in law against her daughter in law, and the daughter in law against her mother in law. And he said also to the people, When ye see a cloud rise out of the west, straightway ye say, There cometh a shower; and so it is. And when ye see the south wind blow, ye say, there will be heat; and it cometh to pass. Ye hypocrites, ye can discern the face of the sky and of the earth; but, how is it that ye do not discern this time? Yea, and why even of yourselves judge ye not what is right?

Luke 12:49–57

7

Kindling Wood: How to Stay on Fire for God

JESUS WANTS YOU and me to be His kindling wood. He wants to start a spiritual fire in a few hearts, that it might spread throughout His church-at-large, into a full-fledged bonfire of a revival.

Jesus first says that He has come to set the world on fire. Second, He says that before He starts that fire, He must go to the cross. And third, He says that He has not come to send peace but, as Matthew puts it, a sword, dividing men according to their relationship to Him (see 10:34). The cross, the fire, and the sword.

He endured the cross. He started the fire. He wields the sword. When He said these things, He faced the baptism of blood on Calvary. "And how am I straitened till it be accomplished!" He was under the terrific urge to accomplish His mission in this world. He didn't come just to live or to teach, but to die and to give His life a ransom for many.

The Cross, the Fire, and the Sword

He's under the constraint of the cross. Our Lord could have set the world on fire after a fashion without the cross. He could have divided men in the Bible sword of loyalty to His cause, without going to Calvary. But He never could have provided redemption. For without shedding of blood, there is no remission of sin.

I'm sure those who wanted to crown Him after He had fed the five thousand with five loaves and two fishes must have said, "If He can do that, He ought to be able to break the yoke of Roman bondage and lead us into the promised land of peace and prosperity. We ought to make a king of Him." But the only crown He ever accepted was the crown of thorns.

The baptism to be baptized with? After the cross, there's a fire. The early church fathers thought this meant the Holy Spirit. Today, they say it means persecution, as the verses that follow would seem to indicate. And yet, the persecution and the division were consequences of the movement begun by the Holy Spirit at Pentecost, so the early fathers and later expositors like McLaren are probably right after all.

Fire is often a symbol of the Holy Spirit. He came at Pentecost with cloven tongues, like as a fire. The world was set on fire then. And all the devices of the devil have never been able to put out the conflagration.

Then, the sword. Our Lord is the great divider. Several times in the Gospels we read that there was a division of the people on account of Him. There always is. He divides families and society and humanity. "He that is not with me is against me, and he that gathereth not with me scattereth abroad" (Matt. 12:30). That disposes forever the myth of the "inactive church member." There is no such thing, because if you're not gathering, you're scattering, and either is activity. When a church member says, "Don't get me wrong. I know I'm not doing anything for the Lord, but I'm not against Him." But he is, because if we're not drawing people to Christ, we're driving people away from Christ, but we're never inactive.

Humanity splits to the right and the left because of my Lord. There's a lot of pleasant talk today about unity and peace and brotherhood that ignores Him. The only true unity is in Him by whom all things consist. And the only true peace with God and of God is in Him who is our peace.

All believers are one brotherhood. Blessed be the tie that binds. And the only brotherhood of man the Bible has anything to say about is the brotherhood of the children of God by faith in Christ Jesus. All who are not identified with Him by the cross and the fire and the sword are outside the fold.

WE'VE PREACHED THE CROSS TO THE WORLD, BUT WE HAVE FAILED TO PREACH IT TO THE CHURCH.

The church today makes pitifully slow progress because her members know so little about the cross, the fire, and the sword. We put crosses on buildings and sing about the cross in worship, but most of our members know next to nothing about what the cross means—for a Christian, at least.

The cross is preached to unbelievers, but the average Christian seems to have never heard about identification with Christ in death and resurrection, although that's what baptism symbolizes. And to most of them, Galatians 2:20 is only a Bible verse, if it's that. We've preached the cross to the world, but we have failed to preach it to the church.

And we've failed likewise with the fire. We're not setting the world on fire today, for all our Bible conferences, Bible teaching ministries, radio preaching, and all the rest of it. Communism is doing it with fire, satanic fire. We have stage fire, strange fire in the religious world, not much spirit fire. No wonder it has been said, "The church has become a *field* for evangelism instead of a *force* for evangelism."

God save us from a synthetic Pentecost!

We say we're depending on the Holy Spirit, but we're so wired up with our own devices, if the fire does not fall from heaven, we can turn on a switch and produce some fire of our own. If there's not the sound of a mighty rushing wind, we have the furnace all set to blow hot air instead. God save us from a synthetic Pentecost!

And since we know so little about the cross and the fire, naturally, we have little experience with the sword. But we have divisions aplenty! Several times in the Gospels it says there was a division of the people on account of Him. But there's another verse that says, "Mark them which cause divisions [among you] . . . and avoid them" (Rom. 16:17).

If you're from a church with division and trouble—"debates, envyings, wraths, strifes, backbitings, whisperings, swellings, tumults" (2 Cor. 12:20), and that entire category the Holy Spirit lists of the sins of the spirit—you might ask, "What caused the division in our church? Is it on account of Him, or is it on account of them?"

If it's on account of Him, it's all right. If it's on account of them, it's all wrong. "Mark them which cause divisions . . . and avoid them." There has never been a time when fundamental

Christianity has been plagued and scandalized by so much bickering and feuds.

I heard of a new organization. They call it the ICGAWA. You know what that means? "I can't get along with anybody." I know some very eligible candidates for that organization!

In a day when we're crying "peace; when there is no peace" (Jer. 6:14), as the Old Testament puts it, or "peace and safety" (1 Thess. 5:3), as the New Testament puts it, we are trying to unify everybody, it seems, instead of calling men to a loyalty to Christ that divides even families. Our Lord came not to send peace, but the sword, and He called men to a cross-bearing discipleship which separates them from the world.

True and False Togetherness

The world is becoming a little more "churchy," and the church is becoming a little more worldly, and the lines are down in this new togetherness. I don't know of any word that I've gotten tired of quicker than this word "togetherness." I'm just worn out with it. And the thing shows no signs of dying.

Of course, there *is* a true togetherness, thank God! Here it is: We represent different churches and fellowships, but we love the Lord. And that kind of togetherness, I like. We have it every time we gather in the name of the Lord.

One of our great Southern preachers used to use a very homely illustration but a good one about this matter. He said, "If you take a bundle of crooked sticks and spread them out, they point in all directions, but if you tie them in a bundle, they have a way of straightening each other out, and they don't look so crooked after all."

When you get the saints together in the unity of the Spirit, we have a way of straightening each other out. I've thought it many times when a congregation is singing. If I had to listen to each person one at a time, my, I'd hate to hear that. But when we get to singing together, we have a way of ironing out all those slurs and flats, those misses and near-misses, that we make all through the song, because we're all working at it. That's the kind of togetherness that I'm in favor of, when we live and pray and sing in unison.

The church upset the world in the early centuries when she was separate and distinct, but she lost her power when Constantine came along and the church was married, that is, the professing church, to the world. And today, while the professing church for the most part fails to travel the way of the cross, the fire, and the sword, all kinds of modern movements are using the very terminology and even techniques of the church to advance their causes. They've stolen our tactics. They talk about a cross, a fire, and a sword. And they emphasize vicarious suffering, and they're aflame with a zeal that defies persecution and prison and death.

Identity of Person, Persuasion, Persecution

Why do we not press the battle to victory with the weapon God gave us to win the heritage of the Christian faith? One reason, as Dr. J.B. Phillips said, is that the church is so prosperous that it's fat and out of breath, and so organized that it's muscle-bound. We're not carrying forth the battle to a good finish because of this sad paralysis that has fallen over us.

We've lost our Christian identity, because we've lost our Christian identification. The word "Christian" is found only three times in the New Testament and each time it's a mark of identification. The disciples were called Christians first at Antioch. They were identified with a person. And then Agrippa said to Paul, "Almost thou persuadest me to be a Christian" (Acts 26:28).

A Christian is a persuader because he's been persuaded. He's persuaded that nothing can separate him from the love of God in Christ. He's persuaded that God will keep that which he has committed unto Him against that day (see 2 Tim. 1:12). And knowing the terror of the Lord, he persuades men.

If you're a Christian, you're identified with a person and a persuasion. And then we read, "If any man suffer as a Christian, let him not be ashamed, but let him glorify God" (1 Pet. 4:16). On this behalf, you're identified with the persecution. How much of that have you known? Do you know anything about this?

Some time ago, the church of which I am a member, the First Baptist of Greensboro, celebrated its 100th anniversary. Dr. Clyde Turner, a former pastor who served for 38 years, wrote a history of the church, in which he said, "Less than a hundred years ago, the members of this church were despised, and their pastor was hissed on the streets." We're not despised now, not with a building worth $1.25 million and a membership of 3,600. It's a typical prosperous church today.

I don't find many churches despised anywhere I go. I don't find pastors being hissed on the street. Somebody has said that if this world is moved for God today, it will be by a persecuted minority scorning the values of this world and living under stringent discipline.

It seems the greatest days of the church were not the days of the cathedrals, but of the catacombs, when Christians were fed to lions in Roman amphitheaters. We've traveled a long way, you know, since the days of the cross, the fire, and the sword. We've lost our identity because we've lost our identification.

Teddy Roosevelt, during the First World War, used to talk about "hyphenated Americans." He was referring to German-Americans who had a divided allegiance, and he said, "If you're an American and something else, you're not an American."

By the same token, if you're a Christian and something else, you're not a Christian. A man who is eighty-five percent faithful to his wife is not faithful at all. There isn't any such thing as part-time devotion to Jesus Christ. If you're not "all out" for Christ, you might as well stay out.

We may have "Christian-plus" church members today, but just as Teddy Roosevelt said that America is not a polyglot boarding house, neither is the church. It's not a catch-all for everybody.

I read the other day a little squib in one of our papers. A certain religious group said, "Oh, we've got room for everybody in our crowd." And after I'd read it all, I said, "That's too much room." That's more room than the New Testament church ever had!

We have too many today who think you get to heaven by being religious instead of by being righteous. They don't seem to understand the kingdom of God is "righteousness, and peace, and joy in the Holy Ghost" (Rom. 14:17)—and righteousness must come before the peace and the joy. Everybody wants the peace and the joy.

The bookstores are loaded with books on serenity and tranquility and peace. But you don't have many people coming to church and asking, "How can I get right and live right and be right and stay right?" It's like a man with a broken arm saying to the doctor, "No, don't set the arm, just give me a shot. I want to feel better, but don't set the arm."

DO WE WANT TO BE PUT RIGHT, OR DO WE JUST WANT TO FEEL BETTER?

A lot of dear people on Sunday mornings say, "I don't want to be put right. Just give me a shot." That's what they get sometimes, and they go out feeling pretty good. Then it wears off, and the trouble's never been ejected.

All of this sits on our own doorstep individually. Churches are made up of people. Let me ask you, and let me ask myself, what do we know about the cross in our experience?

People have heard all of these familiar sayings—that Christ died for sin, that we are dead to sin, that our cross is an "I" crossed out—and all the other things that have been in messages through the years. But do we accept it? Do we agree to it? Do we reckon ourselves dead to sin and alive to God? Do we really consent to death, to the old self-life with all its ambitions and interests?

We've heard it so much we can rattle it off. It has become an easy language with us, but how far have we gone in the experience of it? Alas, too many are just what they've always been, baptized sinners, religious but not righteous. And the cross is only a symbol.

I've watched comfortable Sunday morning congregations sing,

> I take, O cross, thy shadow
> for my abiding place;

I ask no other sunshine than
the sunshine of His face.
content to let the world go by,
to know no pain, no gain nor loss,
my sinful self my only shame,
my glory all the cross.[1]

I have wondered what would happen if that song could leap out of the book and get hold of that crowd just once and live itself out in their experience the rest of the week.

WE'RE NOT SETTING THE WORLD ON FIRE,
BECAUSE WE'RE NOT ON FIRE OURSELVES.

What do we know about the fire? Our Lord didn't stay on the cross. He didn't stay in the tomb. He arose from the dead, and the spirit of God raised Him. We're not only dead to sin; we're alive for the Spirit. At Pentecost, the Spirit came with cloven tongues, and the disciples were set aflame with the zeal that nothing could intimidate or cool.

The average Christian is not only ignorant of the meaning of the cross; he's never been set on fire. Consequently, we're not setting the home and the church and the community and the nation and the world on fire, because we're not on fire ourselves. And of course, if we don't experience the cross and the fire, we know nothing of the sword.

We live in an era of conformity and regimentation. And it's almost the unpardonable sin to be different or to oppose anything. They tell me in our colleges now that debating societies are becoming more and more unpopular because young people today don't like to take sides on issues. They don't like to debate; they don't like to take a firm stand.

It's an Either-Or Universe

Public relations is a major item of interest. The road to success is full of glad-handers, experts in double-talk. We are a neither-nor crowd in a universe that is either-or. Lost or saved, heaven or hell, Christ or Belial.

You can't be neither-nor in God's universe, that's either-or. And yet, I want to give credit where credit is due. I think that I rarely speak anywhere that I don't have in my crowd somebody who has seen the flash of the master's sword. That little woman who slips into church unobserved, who left a godless family at home, who was ridiculed before she started to church, and who will get some more of it when she gets back. She knows what that verse means that says "a man's foes shall be they of his own household" (Matt. 10:36). She has seen the flash of the master's sword.

That student on a pagan campus whose prayer has been, "Lord, make my life a challenge and not a compromise," and who will not lower the flag of faith under pressure nor join in the debauchery to be popular. That student has seen the flash of the master's sword. And that good man who works all day long in a fog of profanity and blasphemy and who turns down the cocktail glass at the boss's party, he knows; he has seen the flash of the master's sword.

Such people don't believe in peace at any price. They follow a Lord who said, "Think not that I am come to send peace on earth: I came not to send peace, but a sword" (10:34).

I tell you, no man can be true to Jesus Christ and be one of the crowd. He's an odd number by the very nature of the case, and he will not be brainwashed into conformity.

Some Adjustment Is Necessary

Of course, there are always minor adjustments and adaptations that any sensible person makes for the sake of the truth, as we become "all things to all men," not to try to please everyone, but that we might "by all means save some" (1 Cor. 9:22). There is a reasonable flexibility. If your backbone stayed rigid all the time, you'd be very uncomfortable!

And yet, I must remind you, on the other hand, the most perfectly adjusted people in the world are all in cemeteries. The sum of the whole matter is this: Our Lord came down here to set the world on fire, and it's on fire, but not with the gospel; it's on fire with world religions; it's on fire with all types of anti-Christian groups. The kind of Christianity most church members have today wouldn't set anything on fire.

I heard of an actress who was very finicky about the temperature in her hotel room, insisting it must always be 72 degrees. This was in the days before air conditioning, so her demand was hard to handle—till somebody had a bright idea.

They took a thermometer, emptied out all the mercury, put red ink in it up to 72 degrees, and hung it in her room, and she was just as happy as could be. She had a little trouble figuring out why there was such a difference between 72 degrees in the winter and 72 degrees in the summer, though!

This Laodicean age is living at a comfortable 72 degrees. But my Lord said this to the lukewarm Laodicean church: "Be zealous therefore, and repent" (Rev. 3:19). The word translated "zealous" actually means "boiling." The church needs to come to a boil.

The time has come to make numbers count. We measure preachers today by how they draw the net, and if they know how to draw the net, they're good. We need somebody who knows how to sort the fish. We've got all kinds of curious creatures in this net. Oh, I know the angels will do it ultimately, but we could do a little separating here in advance if we used our sanctified intelligence.

The Secret to Revival: Start Small

God doesn't move the world with statistics. He moves it with saints, a little Gideon's band that knows something about the cross, the fire, and the sword. Dr. Torrey used to say that to have revival in a church, first let a few members of that church get thoroughly right with God themselves.

Billy Graham has said that if he were a pastor, he would take eight or ten or twelve men and start with them in a prayer meeting. Billy points out that our Lord was not so very successful with big crowds; he did his greatest work with a handful. That's true. Remember, the Revolutionary War started out with minutemen like those heroes who stood there in New England and fired the shot heard round the world.

I'm engaged these days in trying to rally a few "last-minute men." And if God gives me a little more time, I resolve by His grace to engage in trying to gather as never before, not a crowd, but a corporal's guard, who will mean business and be consumed with the zeal for God, His cause, and His house.

When D.L. Moody went to Scotland, the meetings didn't start off well. The crowd built up slowly. Some of the preachers got nervous. They said, "Moody, we'll have to do better than this." Mr. Moody asked them a simple question, "How do you start a fire?"

And anybody who grew up in the country and made fires on a winter morning knows the technique.

Start with Kindling Wood

As a boy I was delegated quite early by my father to be the official fire maker. He said on those cold winter mornings (seemed like it was 2 a.m., but it was a little later), "Get up and make a fire." I learned early in life, it paid to rise on first call. If I waited for second call, that was unfortunate; third call, that was a calamity.

So I rose and made my way into the kitchen, and there I raked off the ashes that had accumulated during the night and hoped there would be some coals underneath, live coals; if there were, that helped a lot. I'd brought in my wood the day before, had my backlog and I had my middle-sized wood, and I had my kindling.

I put my kindling on those live coals and blew and blew till I was blue, and the flame came up. And then I put on my middle-sized wood and had a fire. If I had tried to set that backlog on the fire first, I'd still be down there in Catawba County trying to start a fire. You don't start a fire that way.

Any preacher who is trying first to set on fire that unconverted and undedicated backlog of the majority of the members is wasting time. You don't start a fire that way, and God doesn't start His fires that way. God starts with kindling wood.

Years ago, I went to what is now Gardner-Webb College over in Cleveland County, Boiling Springs High School. They put me in a quartet, the first and last time I was ever in a quartet. (They learned early that I did not belong in quartets.)

I won't forget that first and last venture. I was the bass (and it was *base*, I can assure you!). And we sang a little song:

> My name is Johnny Johnson, I come from Kalamazoo,
> and I'm selling kindling wood to get along.

If you want to help me, just buy my kindling wood,
for I'm selling kindling wood to get along.[2]

I got to thinking about that song the other day: *I'm not selling kindling wood, but I'm gathering kindling wood.* Gathering kindling wood is my business these days. Wherever I go, I try to gather a few young people and older men and women who, under God, are willing to be available, inflammable, and expandable; who are willing to be torches for the truth and fuel for the flame of God.

I know the excuses that you may offer: "I'm so weak; I don't have much money; I don't have gifts; I don't amount to much." Haven't you read again and again of forest fires that burn thousands of acres that started with a spark?

Any of us can be God's kindling wood in our home, our church and our community. Every Christian is usable material, and we're not going to set this world on fire by condemnation of it. We're not going to set the world on fire by conformity to it. We're going to set the world on fire by the combustion of lives ignited by the Spirit of God. If the world ever catches fire again, that's the way it will happen.

The only thing God asks of you is to bring yourself to Him and say,

May Thy rich grace impart
strength to my fainting heart,
my zeal inspire.
As Thou hast died for me,
oh, may my love to Thee,
pure, warm, and changeless be
a living fire.[3]

And she said unto her husband, Behold now,
I perceive that this is an holy man of God,
which passeth by us continually.

Second Kings 4:9

8

A Holy Man of God

MY FIRST PASTORATE was a country charge back in the 1920s. I was a bachelor then, and a pedestrian—I didn't own a car. I didn't buy an automobile until I was 66. I wanted to think it over.

I did a lot of walking in those days. This is the day of the motorist, and any man who walks is viewed with suspicion. You see a man coming down the road now just meditating; you figure he's either out of his head or out of gas, one of the two. And he's such a rarity that dogs bark at him as though they'd seen a ghost. Policemen have been known to follow a pedestrian for blocks to make sure he isn't up to something.

One memory lingers from that pastorate. Along my route there was a grocery store, and the grocer said one day, "Preacher, I want you to know that many a time when things were not going well, I've looked out my store window and I saw you going by, and I felt better."

He didn't elaborate on that, but I've never forgotten it. It's been my prayer that souls along my beat, as I make my way through these years, might be able to say to some small degree what the Shunammite woman said, "I perceive this is a holy man of God who passes by us continually." That ought to be the ambition of every preacher and every Christian in their pilgrimage through this world.

Luke tells us when our Lord was on his way to Jericho, somebody told a blind man, "Jesus of Nazareth passeth by" (18:37). He's still passing by, but not as then. He passes by in His people, and particularly in his preachers.

He has no hands, no feet but ours. And if this world reads the gospel, it'll be the gospel according to you and me, for most of them don't read Matthew, Mark, Luke, and John.

A Holy Man's Secret Strength

In this same pastorate, I remember when I came there, I heard a great deal about an old minister of years before by the name of Josiah Elliott. There had been ministers in that church that went on to prominent pulpits, but I didn't hear much about them, only about Josiah Elliott. I knew he was a very poor man and had given what little he had to help boys through school. But I wondered what was the secret of his strength.

I decided I'd ask my farmer friend, John Brown. He was an unusual character, never in a hurry. He had time to think. I made my way through a cypress swamp to visit him one afternoon. I spent many an afternoon talking with John. He should've been plowing, and I should've been visiting but we'd talk all afternoon. I'd come back the next morning, and we never said, "good morning"; we just took up where we'd left off the day before and went on with our conversation!

I said to him, "John, all I hear around here is Josiah Elliott. You've had preachers that I've heard about, but these people talk only about Josiah Elliott. What was the secret of his strength and the grip that he had on you folks?"

John leaned on the plow handles and thought a moment, as he would often do, and finally said, "He just loved us." Then he went on plowing and left me standing there.

And I made my way back through that cypress swamp while the wood thrush was singing his vespers at the end of a perfect day, and there chimed in my heart something that said, "Though I speak with the tongues of men and of angels and have not charity [love] . . . it profiteth me nothing" (1 Cor.13:1, 3).

I said, "Lord, help me move into the 13th chapter of First Corinthians and settle down for the duration." It's a good place to live. Josiah Elliott was a holy man of God who passed by continually.

1. Elijah Was a Man of God

You will observe that this woman said three things about Elijah: first, he was a "*man of God*" (2 Kings 4:9). A man of God used to be a familiar term, but in this psychedelic age, it appears to indicate a wild and weird and wooly freak. In the Bible, it meant a man who kept company with the Almighty, like Elijah, until he could say to Ahab, "As the Lord of hosts liveth, before whom I stand" (3:14). When you've been accustomed to standing before God, kings don't matter much, and big potentates are just small potatoes when you've been standing in the presence of the Most High.

We think of Enoch, who like Elijah went to heaven without dying. But if he had been buried, I think the epitaph on his tombstone ought to be "He walked with God, he pleased God, and God took him." I'd rather have that on my tombstone than all the laurels this poor world could lay at my feet while I lay in the costliest mausoleum on earth.

A lady asked an old bishop, "What's the matter with me? I've read all the devotional books; I pray; I've taken all the steps they say to take; I've done all the things they say to do—and still, I don't seem to know the Lord. Does God have favorites?"

The old bishop said, "No, not favorites, but God has intimates."

Moses was one of those—"And the LORD spake unto Moses face to face, as a man speaketh unto his friend" (Exod. 33:11). Nobody knows where Moses' grave is. God was his funeral director. But, if he had a monument, what an epitaph that would be!

2. Elijah Was a HOLY Man of God

Moses and Elijah were also *holy* men of God. The Shunammite woman didn't say, "I perceive this is a *famous* man of God"—or *popular*, or *brilliant*, or *successful*—but "a *holy* man of God."

Such words as "holy" and "holiness" have fallen on evil days. They've become a byword—holy this an holy that—and have come to mean fanaticism and emotional excess. Some who have preached the highest standards have sunk the lowest in practice, and we've shied away in horror. We've fallen into a snare of the devil, for every Bible doctrine has been carried to extremes at one time or another.

Just because some folks go into wildfire doesn't mean the rest of us have to live in a deep freeze! We don't have to freeze; we don't have to fry either.

One thing is certain: the Bible is so full of the words "holy" and "holiness" that it takes several pages of a concordance to list them. I undertook to count them some time ago and gave up—from the high priest wearing "Holiness To The Lord" on his mitre (Exod. 28:36), to the four beasts in Revelation, crying "Holy, holy, holy, Lord God Almighty" (Rev. 4:8). This book deserves to be called a Holy Bible.

Whatever you think of holiness, you'd better learn to like it, because the Bible says, "Follow peace with all men, and holiness, without which no man shall see the Lord" (Heb. 12:14).

Some preachers are so anxious to be relevant that they've forgotten how to be reverent.

The world holds a higher standard for us Christians than we hold for ourselves. Clarence True Wilson was a Methodist minister and a leader in the temperance movement; Clarence Darrow, as you may know, was an agnostic lawyer; nevertheless, they were friends. One day Dr. Wilson said to Darrow, "I'm going to speak on holiness at a Methodist meeting."

Darrow said, "What's holiness?"

Dr. Wilson gave him his own definition of holiness: "We believe Christians can live above the power of sin by the Spirit of God."

Darrow thought that one over a moment, and then he said, "Well, if I should ever be a Christian, that's the kind of Christian I'd want to be." He had a higher standard than some of us have for ourselves.

There's a new variety of preacher today who is not interested in being called a holy man of God. He's a Madison Avenue sort of wild man who wants to be called by his first name, just one of the boys, so anxious to be relevant that he's forgotten how to be reverent. If this Shunammite woman had heard Elisha tell some jokes that some preachers tell at civic club luncheons, she would never have given us this text.

Some time ago, I heard it said, "You don't have to wear a halo to be a Christian." Who said you had to wear a halo? You don't have to go around with a great big button saying, "I'm a Christian," or carry a Bible the size of a Chicago telephone directory. But the Bible says Christians belong to a holy nation. And we ought to show by our countenance, conversation, and conduct some of the characteristics of our heavenly nationality.

The Perils of Impurity and Flippancy

Dr. John Henry Jowett advised preachers to "Let thy garments be always *white* [i.e., pure]" (Eccl. 9:8), and warns against a spirit of worldly compromise that "will entice you to wear *gray* [impure] habits when we mix with the businessmen of the congregation and to 'talk *gray*' in conversation with them."

> We are tempted to leave our "noontide lights" behind in our study to move among men with a dark lantern which we can manipulate to suit our company. We pay the tribute of smiles to the low business standard. We pay the tribute of laughter to the fashionable jest. We pay the tribute of easy tolerance to ambiguous pleasures. We soften everything to a comfortable acquiescence. We seek to be "all things to all men" to please all. . . . We're victims of illicit compromise. There's nothing distinctive about our character.[1]

It's a sad day for a preacher when he's mortally afraid somebody will think he is a preacher.

We're living in a day when tragedy has become comedy in America. We're laughing at things that ought to make us cry. And the cause of Jesus Christ has been hurt more by unwise jokesters than by all the infidels. I marvel at the jesting and flippant remarks that I hear sometimes during revivals.

You remember when Uzza tried to steady the ark and dropped dead (1 Chron. 13:7–10)? Have you ever studied what exactly was the sin of Uzza? It must be serious for God to strike a man dead.

Well, for one thing, Uzza was the son of Abinadab, and all his life the Ark had been in his house. It was a familiar piece of furniture. He'd seen it all these years, and the Ark had become just a box. He had lost his regard for the sacredness of it as a symbol of God's presence among His people. Old Matthew Henry says, "Perhaps he affected to show before this great assembly how bold he could make with the Ark, having been so long acquainted with it."

Familiarity, even with that which is most awesome, is apt to breed contempt. Uzza was a Levite, but he wasn't a priest, and only the priest could touch the ark (see Num. 4:15) and only under certain circumstances.

We are priests—we believe in the priesthood of all believers. It's a sad day, my friend, when the ark becomes a box. When you become so familiar with Scripture and worship and the ordinances that you lose your reverence.

Alexander Maclaren said it was a lost sense of awe in the case of Uzza. Nothing is more delicate than a sense of awe. Trifle with it ever so little and it disappears. Watch the average Sunday morning congregation—you don't see much awe out there. What you see is not awe, it's awful! Relevance has become more important than reverence.

You can take God's name in vain in church. You don't have to cuss to take God's name in vain. You can do it when you stand and sing, "My Jesus, I love Thee, I know Thou art mine; for Thee, all the follies of sin I resign"—yet you haven't done it. "Have Thine own way, Lord; hold o'er my being absolute sway"—but you don't mean it.

A tourist in Africa chanced on some boys playing what looked like a game of marbles. He grew near and discovered they were playing marbles with *diamonds!* (It was in South Africa, where in those days diamonds were mined.) Playing marbles with diamonds—we're doing that in the church today.

I read of a girl who was touring Europe; in Vienna, she went to the museum where Beethoven's piano is kept on display. And she sat down and played some rock and roll on it! The old caretaker endured it, and after it was over, he said, "Paderewski was through here some years ago."

"Oh," she said, "and what did he play?"

"Nothing," said the caretaker. "He said he was not worthy to touch Beethoven's piano."

I'm sure that poor little thing must have gone out of there red in the face—if she were capable of embarrassment. It's an awful thing to treat the ark, the holy things of God, like a box, with cheap familiarity.

Is This Real to You?

Someone has said, "There's no greater hindrance to true spirituality than a superficial acquaintance with the language of Christianity from childhood." That sounds like a rather questionable statement. But it caused me to think it over.

I grew up in a Christian home, and I thank God for it. But it's dangerous. I read through the New Testament I don't know how many times when I was a very small boy. I wrote articles for the newspaper when I was nine; I was licensed at eleven, and ordained when I was fifteen. But there came a day when I had to back myself into a corner and say, "Hey, you! Is this real or is it something you've just learned until you can recite it?"

Is this real to you? If we ever have a confrontation with the Holy God, if God ever visits us again in true revival, it'll end this prostitution of holy things, and we'll be red in the face with embarrassment about some of the silly things we've been doing to try to put the gospel over.

IF YOU WANT TO BE POPULAR, PREACH HAPPINESS;
IF YOU WANT TO BE UNPOPULAR, PREACH HOLINESS.

"Oh," you say, "we must relate and communicate to the new age." Well, we're not doing too well with all the new techniques. We're not cutting the mustard. We're preaching happiness instead of holiness. God didn't save you to make you happy—that's a by-product! He saved you to make you holy. You are predestinated to be conformed to the image of God's Son. If you want to be popular, preach happiness; if you want to be unpopular, preach holiness.

"Oh," you say, "but doesn't the Bible tell us, 'If ye know these things, happy are ye if ye do them' (John 13:17)?" Yes; but it's conditioned on two ifs: knowing the *word* of God and doing the *will* of God. And who wants to hear about that now?

There's a price to pay to be a holy man of God. You have to buck the current, because the tide's running the other way.

The Secret of Elisha

What was the secret of Elisha, the holy man of God? It was revealed on the day when Elijah—this prophet who had lived all his life in a furious tempest—was going to heaven in a fiery whirlwind. Elisha made up his mind to be there when it happened. Elijah tried to shake him off at Bethel and at Jericho and at Jordan, but Elisha said, "I will not leave thee" (2 Kings 2:2).

Elisha knew he was the successor to Elijah, and he wanted a double portion of Elijah's spirit (he was not asking for twice as much; he was alluding to an elder son's inheritance). The preacher that God honors today is the man who has made up his mind to have the best God has for him, and will not be put off with anything less.

Along the road that day, there were some seminary students. And they knew something was going to happen. They inquired about it. Fifty of them stood to view it afar off, but nothing happened to them.

That's as close as some people ever get to a double portion of God's blessing. They hear about it and talk about it, and they're in the vicinity, but they never see the chariots of fire and Elijah's mantle is not for them. Beloved, it is not enough to live in the neighborhood of a miracle. Holy men of God don't live on hearsay and secondhand experiences.

There are plenty of schools of the prophets these days along the roadsides, gossiping like these young prophets did. But, it's only once in a while that an Elisha says, "I'm going through to a double portion into the prophet's mantle."

Do you remember what he said to those preachers? "Hold ye your peace" (2:3). Men who are in dead earnest don't engage in idle chatter with roadside reverends. Elijah's translation wasn't a subject for idle speculation; it wasn't a temporary excitement. Elisha knew it was for him the opportunity of a lifetime, and if he blew it, he'd be an ordinary preacher the rest of his days.

The preacher who's out for God's best doesn't have any time to waste on bystanders. Some stop at Bethel, and some stop at Jericho and never get to Jordan because they talk it over with the schools of the prophets.

The preacher who is out for the prophet's mantle will do well to say to all these seminarians who rarely talk about it, "Hold your peace." Don't you let anybody stop short of God's best for you. He went the distance that makes the difference.

"How Fer Have You Went?"

In the North Carolina foothills where I live, we used to have on the radio on Sunday morning a lot of little mountain preachers and country preachers, and they loved God and won souls. They did terrible things to the King's English sometimes, but they were great souls.

One morning, one of those old boys was preaching forth on the text, "He went a little farther" (Matt. 26:39). And every once in a while in the sermon, he'd fairly blast the elements by yelling, "How fer have you went?" Well, I wouldn't have minded it if he'd said it just once, but every once in a while, "How fer have you went?" I was sitting there all alone, listening to him on the radio, and finally, I couldn't take it any longer. I yelled back at him, "Brother, you done went too fer now!" But it is quite a question.

In the book of Ruth, when Naomi told her daughters-in-law to return to Moab, "Orpah kissed her mother in law;

but Ruth clave unto her. . . . And Ruth said, Intreat me not to leave thee" (Ruth 1:14, 16). We've got a lot of saints today who give the Lord a kiss once in a while. But God wants people who say with Ruth, "Wither thou goest, I will go; and where thou lodgest, I will lodge: thy people shall be my people, and thy God my God" (1:16). Ruth went on to be the great-grandmother of David and an ancestor of Jesus Christ.

Judas betrayed the Lord not with a slap, but with a kiss. And Jesus Christ is being betrayed more today with a kiss than with a slap. We notice the slaps and say, "Isn't that awful?" But plenty of people give Him a kiss of respect and never follow Him. Have you gone the distance that makes the difference?

I was preaching to a crowd of preachers in East Tennessee in the mountains some time ago. I got up every morning before breakfast to climb one of those mountains, because I still can get up them. But it was a little rough, and when I got about halfway up, discretion told me that since I'm not quite as young as I used to be, I ought to settle for that.

But I saw a light place up there among the trees, and I said, "I believe if I reach it, there'll be a view," and I made it. I was rewarded with a panorama that I'll never forget.

As I stood there that early morning and looked out upon that unforgettable sight, I said, "The difference is worth the distance." It is that extra mile of prayer, that extra time with your Bible, that extra season of communion that makes the difference.

Old William Law said, "Who am I to lie folded up in the bed late of a morning when the farmers have gone about their work and I'm so far behind with my sanctification?" We're all behind with that.

Jim Elliott, before he went to Ecuador, said, "I went to a friend's house last night to look at television, and God laid on my heart Psalm 119:37, 'Turn away mine eyes from beholding vanity.'" He writes like one of the old mystics.

It's that extra mile that lets us sing,

> My heart has no desire to stay
> where doubts arise, and fears dismay.
> Though some may dwell where these abound,
> my prayer, my aim is higher ground.[2]

I'm not going to label that experience. We argue about it, whatever you want to call it. It's that extra mile that gets through to God's best.

3. Elijah Was Passing By Continually

And then, this Shunammite woman said, "This is a man of God, a holy man of God that passeth by us continually." Elisha didn't hide in a cave and polish his halo. He walked among men. Our Lord didn't spend his days lecturing in some secluded spot "far from the madding crowd's ignoble strife." He went about doing good. Jesus was always passing by, and so must we. Because, if we say we abide in Him, we ought to walk as He walked (see 1 John 2:6). Our walk must match our talk.

Elisha was available to everybody, from kings to commoners, and they all beat a path to his door. He solved the water problem at Jericho. He put a prophet's wife in the oil business. He raised the Shunammite's son, healed Naaman of his leprosy, purified the poison in the pot, recovered lost axe-heads, relieved the famines, anointed Jehu, and led the Syrians blind into Samaria.

And after he died and long after he'd been buried, they lowered somebody else's corpse on the bones of that old prophet, and that fellow came back to life. Why, even his corpse woke up the dead!

I tell you, that old preacher had a lot of vitality in his system. He had more power dead than the rest of us have living. He made a trail of blessings.

Other Men of God Who Passed By Continually

Some time ago I spent a few weeks in the Ozarks. I love springtime in the mountains. And an old mountain missionary took me way back in the hills to show me some of his work, and he told me about his predecessor.

"He did a great work here," he said "He used to drive an old ramshackle automobile down these crooked trails. And he had sort of an amplifier rigged up in his car and he'd come down those crooked roads singing at the top of his voice, 'I know the Lord will make a way for me. I know the Lord will make a way for me. If I live a holy life, shun the wrong and do the right, I know the Lord will make a way for me.'" And they say the mountain folks would stop whatever they were doing and listen, and then they'd say, "That's the missionary going home." That's a great way to go home, brother. That's the way I want to go home. And I want somebody to be able to say along the way, "It was a holy man of God who passed by us."

There was another character that used to be around Moody Bible Institute, and I thought so much of him, Homer Hammontree. Homer Hammontree grew up in little old Greenback, Tennessee. He sang the gospel all over the land and taught music. Out of the hills he came, and back to the hills he went. All his life, he was just a big old Tennessee boy. Well, last fall, I was preaching in Johnson City and Knoxville and Maryville, and I said to the preacher, “Where is Greenback, Tennessee?”

He said, “It’s not far from here.”

And I said, “Let’s go over there.” And I found a country cemetery and Hammontree’s grave. He never married. He lay there alone beside a big shade tree. And on that tombstone were the words, “The world passeth away and the lusts thereof: but he that doeth the will of God abideth forever” (1 John 2:17).

The last time I heard Hammontree sing, he and Paul Beckwith sang, “The Story of Jesus Will Never Grow Old.” It’s good to grow old singing a song that won’t grow old, an ageless theme that the years cannot dim, nor time outdate. “He that doeth the will of God”—that’s success, that’s fulfillment.

When it’s my time to go to be with the Lord, it’s my wish that all the lives I’ve touched along the road might be able to say to some degree, “I perceive that this was a holy man of God who passed by us continually.”

I am come that they might have life, and that they might have it more abundantly.

John 10:10

Thanks be to God, which giveth us the victory through our Lord Jesus Christ.

First Corinthians 15:57

Christ liveth in me.

Galatians 2:20

For to me to live is Christ.

Philippians 1:21

This is the victory that overcometh the world, even our faith.

First John 5:4

9

Living as a "V" Christian

DURING THE Second World War, Winston Churchill stood in the midst of the wreckage of London and held up two fingers in a "V" sign of victory, and that became a well-known symbol. Almost 2000 years ago, Jesus Christ stood in the wreckage of this sin-cursed world and said to his disciples, "In the world, ye shall have tribulation: but be of good cheer; I have overcome the world" (John 16:33).

You don't get to heaven by living like Jesus. You can't do it by yourself. You don't get to heaven by living for Jesus, as you would espouse some other cause.

You don't get to heaven by being a "Christ-firster" either. I'm a little leery of these folks who say they put Christ first, because I have a sneaking suspicion, they put a lot of other things next, and He really is Alpha and Omega; he's the whole thing, start and finish.

So much of our modern Christianity is dead—a form of godliness without the power. It's like the church at Sardis. It didn't have a reputation of being a dead church; it was thought of as a live church, but my Lord didn't think so.

New Testament Christianity Is Vital

New Testament Christianity ought to be *vital.* It ought to be alive. I read some time ago these words: "The town bell rang at noon, and the church gave up her dead." It was on Sunday and a rather sad comment, it seemed to me. When so many of our meetings start at 11:00 sharp and end at 12:00 dull, there's something tragically wrong.

THE CORPSE NEVER LOOKED SO GOOD,
BUT IT'S STILL A CORPSE.

There's the appearance of life, but a mortician can make a dead man look better than he ever looked while living. We have programs for revitalizing churches, and after they get through, the corpse never looked so good, but it's still a corpse.

Daniel Webster made this terrific comment about the Constitution of the United States. You can take out the word "government" and put "church" in there, and it still holds.

> You may look on a Government, and see it possess all the external modes of Freedom, and yet find nothing of the essence, the vitality, of freedom in it; just as you may contemplate an embalmed body, where art hath preserved proportion and form, amidst nerves without motion, and veins void of blood.[1]

Only Daniel Webster could have said it like that. And that can be the condition of Christianity. But it's Christ, and modern Christianity has only as much life in it as it has Christ in it.

There's only been one Christian life lived, anyhow. He lived it. That's the only Christian life that's been lived, but He lives it again in you and in me, if we give Him our consent and our cooperation. We preach Him as Savior and we preach Him as Lord, but I wonder if we preach Him enough as Life. And so we have a lot of Christians suffering from low vitality and spiritual anemia.

To the average church member, Christianity is a matter of church on Sunday. One never gets the impression that here's somebody who is day by day an example of the outliving of the inliving Christ. And the fruit of the Christian is another Christian. Normally, the living can propagate their kind. Spiritual corpses don't produce spiritual children; it must be *vital.*

New Testament Christianity Is Vocal

New Testament Christianity ought to be *vocal.* It ought to have something to say. I believe in an articulate faith. And we've lost our voice today, and so much of the church is like arctic rivers frozen at the mouth—no testimony.

When I was a boy, we used to have an old-fashioned country doctor. His hours were twenty-four a day, seven days a week. Today, you can't get sick on certain days in the week; the doctor is not available. But old Dr. Ford was. He would come to our house, sometimes late at night—hadn't had a bit of sleep, shoes untied (no time to tie them), a bag so full of pills that it looked like it might explode at any moment. And the first thing he'd say would be, "Let me see your tongue."

That's a good way to examine a Christian. You tell me what you're talking about, and I can tell a lot about you. We are to have a vocal faith.

Christian experience begins with (vocal) repentance: "Take with you words, and turn to the LORD" (Hosea 14:2). Faith is vocal: "If thou shalt confess with thy mouth the Lord Jesus" (Romans 10:9). Praise is vocal: "By him therefore let us offer the sacrifice of praise to God continually, that is, the fruit of our lips giving thanks to his name" (Hebrews 13:15). Testimony is vocal: "Let the redeemed of the LORD say so" (Psalm 107:2).

What's down in the well will come up in the bucket. And if you really have something down here in your heart, you'll talk about it. You talk about what you're interested in.

Some young fellow who's in love, if he knows you pretty well, he doesn't talk to you long until he gets out a picture of his girl to show to you. (And then you know love is blind when you see the picture!) But he's in love, and what's down in the well comes up in the bucket. It's vocal.

New Testament Christianity Is Visible

Then, it ought to be *visible*. It shows up in conduct. It shows up in how you live. "When they saw the boldness of Peter and John" (Acts 4:13). That word "boldness" is found three times in that chapter—a boldness seen by the world when they saw the boldness of Peter and John.

Then they had a prayer meeting, and prayed, "Grant unto thy servants that with all *boldness* . . ."—that's what got them into trouble to begin with, and here they were praying for more of it!—"that with all boldness we may speak thy word" (4:29). And then they had an earthquake: "the place was shaken . . . and they spake the word of God with boldness" (4:31). Seen by the world, sought by the church, supplied by the Spirit. And that's the way it ought to be.

Christianity is vocal, but the talk must be evident in the walk. "He that saith he abideth in him"—that's the vocal part—"ought himself also to walk, even as He walked" (1 John 2:6)—that's the visible part. We're to love the Lord our God, and we're to love our neighbor (see Matt. 22:37–39).

You can't tell whether a man loves God by looking at him, but you can tell whether he loves his neighbor by what he does. For example, Jesus said, "I was an hungred, and ye gave me meat: I was thirsty, and ye gave me drink" (Matt. 25:35).

Of course, you can have a visible practice of good deeds without vital faith, and that's the danger of social action without spiritual reality. But faith without works is dead.

We are epistles, known and read of all men. And if we're going to be read, if you're going to read something, there has to be something you can see. So, we need an outbreak of vital, vocal, visible Christianity.

New Testament Christianity Is Vivid

Christianity ought to be *vivid*—as TV says sometimes, "live and in color." There isn't anything dull and drab about our faith. It's divine electricity!

On the mount of transfiguration, my Lord's face shown as the sun and his raiment was white as light. That's vivid!

And I don't wonder that John fell down as if dead on the isle of Patmos when he beheld the glorified Lord. John had seen Jesus in more different ways than anybody else has ever seen Him: saw Him in the flesh, saw Him in his resurrection body, but he has one on the other disciples, saw Him glorified on Patmos, and that knocked him out.

He didn't lay his head on the breast of Christ on that day, and I don't wonder, because I read in Revelation 1:12–16,

> I turned to see the voice that spake with me. And being turned, I saw seven golden candlesticks; and in the midst of the seven candlesticks one like unto the Son of man, clothed with a garment down to the foot, and girt about the paps with a golden girdle. His head and his hairs were

> white like wool, as white as snow; and his eyes were as a flame of fire; and his feet like unto fine brass, as if they burned in a furnace; and his voice as the sound of many waters. And he had in his right hand seven stars: and out of his mouth went a sharp twoedged sword: and his countenance was as the sun shineth in his strength.

Now, that's vivid! No wonder John couldn't take it. I have a feeling that if we had one little glimpse of our glorified Lord some Sunday morning at church, just one little glimpse, we wouldn't go out saying some of the silly things we say a minute after we get out the door.

Christianity is not a pale and colorless faith. It's radiant and exciting. We're the salt of the earth, and that gives taste and flavor; we're the light of the world, and that gives brightness and cheer. Every page of the Acts of the Apostles is a sensational page.

But the salt has lost its savor; the light's under a bushel. The experience has become a performance and the vivid, God help us, have become livid sometimes—ashen and pallid, ghastly and ghostly. Christians used to shout in the aisles; now they go to sleep in the pews, listening to the same gospel. And when it becomes livid, it's because it's lost its vitality; when it has no life, it doesn't have any luster.

New Testament Christianity Is Victorious

Finally, Christianity is victorious. God gives us the victory. This is the victory. Today, we are hearing about peace without victory. We've had two wars without victory—Korea and Vietnam. Paul Harvey says, "We were afraid to win them and ashamed to lose them." And that's about the size of it.

Douglas MacArthur said, "In war, there is no substitute for victory." There is no such thing as peaceful coexistence with communism, or with the world, the flesh, or the devil. These things are cancers, and you don't have peaceful coexistence with cancer. If you don't get the cancer, the cancer gets you. Christianity wasn't meant to live with a truce.

Jesus Christ conquered sin; God's not dead; the church hasn't failed; the gates of hell won't prevail against it. I am not presiding at the funeral of a dead deity, and I'm not reading the obituary of a lost cause.

We have a spell of "re-thinking" every once in a while—re-thinking Genesis, re-thinking inspiration, re-thinking the resurrection—and it makes me a little uneasy. It doesn't need re-thinking; it needs re-living. And when you announce that we're going to have a group of "experts" re-think our position, it gives the impression that we're not quite certain about our position.

We ought to take the initiative, like that old captain whose band was surrounded by the enemy. A subordinate said, "They've got us surrounded."

He replied, "Good, don't let one of them escape."

That's the spirit in which we ought to face the foe that we're up against today.

No, the Dam's Not About to Break

Out West an engineer built a wonderful dam, and a great reservoir of water gathered behind it. And the engineer had built a cottage down below it. One day a rumor got out that the dam was about to break. People began scurrying in all directions, and somebody came up to him and said, "Get going, the dam is about to break."

And he asked, "What dam?"

They said, "The one that you built is about to break."

He leaned back in his chair and said, "That dam won't break. I know what's in that dam."

And you know, they're running around now saying the old faith is about to break and the old gospel won't hold. I don't know what you're going to do. You can run if you want to. I'm staying. That dam won't break. It won't break till Calvary breaks. It won't break till the resurrection breaks. It won't break till John 3:16 breaks. It's the rock of ages. I'm not nervous. It's not going to break.

Get Ready for "V" Day!

I'm looking for "V" day, getting ready for the greatest celebration of all time, when Jesus Christ comes back to consummate His triumph. But for a Christian, any day is "V" day.

When we're passing through great trial and testing, we are inclined to wait till the storm is over and the battle ends to celebrate victory. We lift our weary heads and our tear-dimmed eyes to some blessed day on ahead or even to heaven. We groan, and that's all right.

Paul groaned, and creation groans, and the Holy Spirit groans when He prays for us. But we plod through gloomy days and sleepless nights looking for that light at the end of the tunnel.

But if you know my Lord, today is "V" day. This is the victory. I am with you all the days, including this one, as miserable as it is. And that victory was won at Calvary in the open grave. This is the only war I know of that started out with the victory. We're operating from our Waterloo, and we're just engaged in mopping-up operations.

We're living between two "V" days: the "V" day of grace and the "V" day of glory, the "V" day of the cross and the "V" day of the crown. And when the battle is the fiercest and no end seems in sight, if you can walk by faith that day in spite of feelings that drain the blood from your lips and in spite of circumstances that laugh at you and tell you there's nothing to it and that you're a hypocrite; if you can rise above all that and still walk by faith, that's victory now.

THANK GOD YOU CAN LIVE ABOVE THE CIRCUMSTANCES!

The war wasn't over when Churchill held up his two fingers. He was in the middle of it.

I've been passing through a time of great trial for three months. And I bring you good news. I'm not giving you (or myself) a cute little pep talk—I don't know what the outcome will be of my trial. I don't know when the clouds will lift and the sun will break through, but I saw a little word on a preacher's desk the other day: "I believe in the sun when the sun doesn't shine. I believe in God when God is silent."

I know that sun is still up there when it isn't shining. Sometimes God says yes; sometimes God says no; and sometimes God just doesn't say. And the hardest part of the road is that part where God doesn't say, and you have to wait.

I'm not living *under* the circumstances—that will crush you. And I'm not trying to fight my way *through* the circumstances—that will kill you. Thank God you can live *above* the circumstances! I see not yet all things put under Him (see Heb. 2:8). The devil is still here, and sin is still here, and disease is still here, and heartache and heartbreak; but I see

Jesus! I don't have to stand "on Jordan's stormy banks . . . / and cast a wishful eye."[2] I can dwell in Beulahland now.

One of these days, I'll stand before the throne complete. I'm not complete now—and yet, I am complete in Him. I've just been out in Kentucky where the novel that some older folks read a long time ago, *The Little Shepherd of Kingdom Come*, was written, and out there they call it "Kingdom Come Country." I wrote a book and titled it, *Kingdom Come*. We're living in "Kingdom Come."

The kingdom came with Jesus. He announced it. We're living in it now. It has come, and it's still coming. It's a kingdom of righteousness, peace, and joy. Now, it's not visible, but one of these days my Lord is going to set it up and you will see it; it'll be visible. Righteousness first, mind you. Some people don't care for righteousness. They'll buy books about peace and joy more than they will about righteousness.

I've Read the Last Page

When I was a boy, I used to read a lot of stories, a lot of novels, and I always read the last page first. I wanted to find out what happened. Then, I'd start back at page one. Sometimes, it looked like the hero wouldn't make it through the next page. But I'd say, "Cheer up, friend, I know the end from the beginning; I've read the last page." I've got a Bible here this morning that has no devil on the first page and no devil on the last page. Aren't you glad you've got one book that disposes of the devil? Now, in the middle of it, it looks like he's got things going his way.

But ah, oh devil, you can strut across that page all you want to, but your goose is cooked from the start. I've read the last page, and I know what's on it. I'm not out to win the victory. It's been won. I'm standing with my Lord in His triumph. I'm not here to explain the world; I'm not here to enjoy it; I'm not here to endure it. I'm here to overcome it, and this is what overcomes.

During the war, I was in a meeting with Dr. J.B. Phillips of Baltimore, in his Presbyterian church. The meeting closed on Sunday and I was due to start with Bob Cook in LaSalle, Illinois, on Monday night. Trains were not keeping very close schedules, and somebody said, "You'll never make it in time."

And I said, "Oh, yes, the Lord wants me to speak Monday night over there at 7:30. I think I'll make it."

The next morning, I looked across in the pullman and over there was the Secretary of War. And of course, he didn't know me, but I knew him. They say a cat can look at a king, so I looked. He was on his way to Chicago to make a big speech, and I was on the way to LaSalle to start a meeting.

He sent word up to the engineer, "We've got to make Chicago on time." And we did; we didn't even hesitate in most of those towns. We went right on through. But I had the time of my life. I thought, *This big shot thinks they're hurrying up this train to get him to Chicago to speak; the Lord is getting me to LaSalle to start my meeting Monday night.* Why, I had the government working for me that time!

My Lord is on His way to set up His kingdom. He's running on schedule. He may seem slow, but he'll never be late. And when he reaches that destination, you'll be there too, if you're on the same train. That's victory! It's a great railway line. It starts at victory, and it ends at victory. And, thank God, it's victory all the way.

And when he had found him, he brought him unto Antioch. And it came to pass, that a whole year they assembled themselves with the church, and taught much people. And the disciples were called Christians first in Antioch.

Acts 11:26

10

Marks of a Christian

THE WORD "CHRISTIAN" is found only three times in the New Testament. And each time, it is a mark of identification. Christians have lost their identity today, because they've lost their identification.

A Person, a Persuasion, and a Persecution

In Acts 11:26, the disciples were called Christians first at Antioch. A Christian is a "Christ"-ian. He's somebody in whom Christ lives. So, first of all, he's identified with a person. In Acts 26:28, "Agrippa said unto Paul, Almost thou persuadest me to be a Christian."

A Christian is identified with a persuasion. He's persuaded that God is able to keep that which he's committed unto Him against that day. He is persuaded that nothing can separate him from the love of God in Christ, and knowing the terror of the Lord, he persuades men. He's a persuader, because he's been persuaded. In First Peter 4:16 we read, "Yet if any man suffer as a Christian, let him not be ashamed; but let him glorify God on this behalf."

A Christian is identified with a persecution. The Bible says, "All that will live godly in Christ Jesus shall suffer persecution" (2 Tim. 3:12). It doesn't say some or most; it says all. Now, let me ask you, have you ever suffered any persecution as a Christian?

We sing, "To that old rugged cross I will ever be true, / its shame and reproach gladly bear."[1] How much of that have you ever borne? What is it? What is the reproach of the cross?

It's not just ordinary trouble, because everybody has trouble. Some people, when they have a headache, they think they're "bearing their cross." That's not your cross. You can kill that with an aspirin tablet!

What is the cross of Christ? The reproach of the cross is the trouble you have that you wouldn't have if you weren't a Christian. How much trouble have you had that you wouldn't have if you weren't a Christian—persecution, reproach, scorn? A Christian is identified with a person, a persuasion, and a persecution. That's the way to identify him.

Mistaken Identity

Some time ago, a little boy asked his father, "What is a Christian?" His father told him according to the Bible just what a Christian is.

Then the little fellow asked, "Have I ever seen a Christian?"

I don't blame him. Sometimes I think the traveler has been lost in the baggage. We've become so occupied with the paraphernalia that we fail to identify the Christian himself.

I read of a housewife who heard a knock at the door, and a stranger was standing there and he asked her ever so abruptly, "Do you know Jesus Christ?" She didn't know what to say. She stood there and stared at him, and finally closed the door in his face.

When her husband came home that night, she told him what had happened, and he said, "Well, why didn't you tell him that you're the teacher of the Ladies Bible Class and president of the Women's Missionary Society?"

"That's not what he asked me," she replied. "He asked me, 'Do you know Jesus Christ?'"

You can be a lot of things and not know Jesus Christ. A Bible Christian is one who knows Jesus as a personal Savior and is living by faith in and in fellowship with Him.

A Christian is saved. Acts 2:47 says, "And the Lord added to the church daily such as should be saved." It doesn't say all that were sincere or sanctimonious.

Conviction, Repentance, Faith, Confession

Salvation is a four-fold experience. There must be *conviction* of sin by the Holy Spirit through the Word of God. There must be the general conviction of "all have sinned" and the personal conviction of "I have sinned"—that I've broken God's law, I'm under condemnation, and the wrath of God abides on me.

You don't hear much these days about the sinfulness of the human heart. That's not because we have any less of it.

I heard about an old preacher who gave a great message on the depravity of the human heart. Someone came up after the service and said, "I just can't swallow this depravity of the human heart you've been preaching about."

The old preacher replied, "You don't have to swallow it. It's already in you."

The Christian has been *repentant* towards God, which means turning with a broken and contrite heart from sin and self to the Savior. Paul preached both repentance *and* faith, and "What therefore God hath joined together, let not man put asunder" (Matt.19:6).

Some people ask which comes first, repentance or faith. Spurgeon used to say, "That would be like saying when John Smith walks in the door, which came in first, John or Smith?" They accompany each other.

IT'S THROUGH FAITH IN JESUS THAT WE'RE GIVEN POWER TO BECOME THE SONS OF GOD.

There must be *faith* in Jesus Christ, a simple faith that receives Him into the heart as the Son of God made sin for us, who bears our sins in His own body, and by whose blood we're cleansed from sin. It's through faith in Jesus that we're given power to become the sons of God.

George Whitefield, the great preacher, was asked, "Why do you preach so much on 'Ye must be born again?'" And he answered, "Because ye must be born again!"

I was in the state of Iowa many years ago, in a meeting out in a farm home one day, and a little girl was singing some choruses for us. And she undertook to sing, "God has blotted them out." She couldn't quite pronounce "blotted," so she sang, "God has *blooded* them out." That's good theology! And that's what He's done, with the blood of His Son.

If we've been *convicted*, if we've *repented*, and if we've *believed*, we must *confess* with the mouth before men the outward experience—the outward expression of an inward experience—by which "the redeemed of the LORD say so" (Ps. 107:2).

We've got too many silent Christians today. They're like arctic rivers—frozen at the mouth. The Bible says, "With the heart man believeth . . . and with the mouth confession is made" (Rom. 10:10).

Some people say, "Well, my grandmother was a good Christian, and she never said anything about it publicly." But it's not a matter of how good your grandmother was! The Bible says, ". . . with the mouth, confession is made."

Conviction, repentance, faith, and confession—if it takes these four things, that's miles away from just signing a card and joining a church. The greatest experience on earth—when darkness turns to day, bondage turns to freedom, and the angels are set singing—is because the sinners come home.

Marks of Identification

A Christian is not only saved, he ought to be sure he's saved. We've got too many people who don't know if they're saved or not. No born-again, blood-washed believer has any business going through this world as an animated question mark, up one day and down the next, and never able to stand at any time or place with the full assurance of salvation.

The Word of God says we can know whom we believe (see 2 Tim. 1:12). We can know that we have eternal life (see 1 John 5:13), that He abides in us by the Spirit (see 3:24), and that we have passed from death unto life, because we love the brethren (see 3:14). There are certain marks of identification in the Bible for a Christian.

A Christian Is Righteous

The Christian is a new creature. He does not commit sin; that is to say, he does not make sinning his practice. When you see a man who makes sinning his practice, he's never been saved. The Christian may *fall into* sin; he may be overtaken by a fault. But just as a farmer is a man who farms, a sinner is a man who sins; that's his business. When a man makes sinning his business, he's a sinner.

A Christian does righteousness. He overcomes the world. There are two ways of proving you've been born again and two ways of proving you're born the first time. To prove you were born, you could produce a birth certificate, but the very fact you're here tonight is evidence that you've been born.

To prove you were born again, you could give your testimony and tell us when you were saved. That's one way. But the fact that you're living a Christian life, if you are, that's evidence. And in this day of human question marks, we need a lot of living exclamation points who've got the kinks taken out of them and who know that they know that they're saved, because God said so—and God saying so makes it so.

A Christian Is Sound in Doctrine

Every Christian ought to be sound. They continued steadfastly in the apostles' doctrine; they are the Christians. We've come to a time when some people say, "It doesn't matter much what you believe, as long as everybody is getting along with each other." We've come to a day of trumpets with an uncertain sound, and the less a preacher is sure of the more sense some people think he has.

At a conference years ago in Kentucky, Dr. George Ragland told us about a rather illiterate old lady out in the country who had a habit of using the expression, "nor nothing," instead of saying, "not anything."

One Sunday, they had a modernistic preacher there, and he preached a little lavender rose water sermonette that started nowhere and ended in the same place. And after it was over, the old lady came down and shook hands with him and said, "Sure did enjoy your sermon. It didn't have no doctrine in it nor nothing."

When a sermon doesn't have doctrine, it doesn't have anything in it. And we're paying for this today; folks are on milk when they ought to be on meat. I thank God the blood makes faith and the word makes sure, and as we continue in the apostles' doctrine, we're sound, steadfast, and unmovable.

I believe in being dogmatic about what you believe, not "bulldogmatic," but dogmatic. When I get sick and go to a doctor, I want him to tell me what's the matter with me. I want him to be dogmatic. I don't want him to say, "Well, it could be this and it might be that. We'll give you these pills, and if they don't kill you, we'll try something else." I want him to be dogmatic.

When I get on the train, what few of them are left, or get on a plane, I don't want the engineer or pilot to throw away his instructions. I want him to be dogmatic. I want him to know where he's going and head that way.

When I go to church, I don't want a preacher to stand up and say, "You must repent, as it were," or "believe in a measure and be damned to some extent." I want him to be dogmatic.

A Christian Is Surrendered

A Christian ought to be surrendered. Romans 6:13 "Yield yourselves to God." Abraham is the Bible's example of the walk of faith. One day God said to Abraham, "I want you to give up Ishmael." Ishmael was the worst thing in Abraham's life, born out of the will of God, born of the will of the flesh. God took Ishmael, and he never did come back. Then God said, "I want Isaac."

Isaac was the best thing in Abraham's life, born in the will of God, born of faith. God took Isaac, but He gave him back. God wants the Ishmaels in your life, the bad things that He may take them away and they never come back. He also wants the good things, that He may give them back—sanctified and meet for the Master's use (see 2 Tim. 2:21).

All the trouble over in the Middle East is because Ishmael and Isaac started it a long time ago. All of the warfare through the years, that is still going on, is because two half-brothers never could divide the land up right.

It's still going on. You have war over there, and you will continue to have it—we have to admit it. I'm sympathetic with the Arabs who are suffering; I'm sympathetic when anybody suffers. But, Ishmael was a mistake to begin with. He was not in the will of God.

We need to proclaim a day of repentance in our churches for the songs we sing that we don't mean. Sometimes I think more lies can be told behind a hymn book than almost any other way—and look so innocent doing it.

> My Jesus, I love Thee; I know Thou art mine;
> For Thee all the follies of sin I resign.[2]

Some of the people who sing that have a wagonload of follies they never have given up and don't mean to.

> Have Thine own way, Lord, have Thine own way;
> Hold over my being absolute sway.[3]

I almost have chills when I see a congregation sing that. "Absolute" means 100 percent. When a Christian is absolutely surrendered to God, that's asking God to take over—lock, stock, and barrel.

> Take my life and let it be
> consecrated, Lord, to Thee.[4]

How about that one? The way some folks live, they seem to think it means, "Take my life and let it be—just lay my life up on a shelf somewhere, Lord, just let it be."

That's not what it says! Don't stop in the middle of the sentence. "Take my life and let it be *consecrated*." And if we meant what we were singing, it'd take care of a lot of our problems about personal conduct.

I believe our greatest trouble with that hymn lies in the verse that says, "Take my will and make it Thine." There's where the battle is fought—not in your emotions, not in your feelings, but in your will. "Whosoever will, let him come" (see Rev. 22:17). You give God your will and He'll get your hands, feet, and voice, and your silver and gold. But too many people have never made up their minds to serve Jesus Christ.

A Christian Is Separated

A Bible-believing Christian is a separated Christian. "Come out from among them, and be ye separate" (2 Cor. 6:17). The early Christians were peculiar people. Today they're a popular people. The devil tried to put the church out of business by persecution and couldn't. You can't kill a church by persecution, instead it will keep on growing. Every time you cut off one head, two more come up.

For countless Christians, church membership means less than ever. Too many church members are trying to take a spiritual sunbath when they need surgery. The Bible says, "Abhor that which is evil" (Rom. 12:9) and "Ye that love the LORD, hate evil" (Ps. 97:10). The fear of the Lord is to hate evil, and yet we flirt with evil and wink at the devil and serve our own god.

The Bible teaches that churches and Christians ought to separate from four things:

1. the world (see 2 Cor. 6:14–17; James 4:4; 1 John 2:15–17);
2. immoral Christians (see 1 Cor. 5:1–8);
3. false doctrines (see 2 John 10, 11);
4. church disturbers (see Rom. 16:17).

Don't misunderstand me. I'm not preaching a "don't" religion. Some people are only as good as "trying not to be bad" can make them. The Pharisees, for instance, were separate. They wouldn't even eat an egg that had been laid on the Sabbath, and that's going too far; but they weren't surrendered to the Lord. So I'm not just telling you to quit this and quit that.

A Christian Is Spirit-Filled

A Christian should also be Spirit-filled. Sam Jones, the great evangelist, was a drunkard and God saved him. He said, "God said to me, 'Sam, you've got your pockets full of dirt. Throw out the dirt, and I'll fill them with diamonds.'" Sam said, "Who wouldn't give up dirt for diamonds?"

Thomas Edison put old-fashioned oil lamps out of business. How did he do it? He didn't go around with a sledgehammer and smash all of them. He just invented the electric light. And when the electric light came along, out went lamps. When you get the light of God in your heart, out will go all these things that don't belong in a Christian's life.

We're not going to have peace in today's world through education and legislation. A Spirit-filled American and a Spirit-filled Russian will get along. A Spirit-filled white man and a Spirit-filled black man will get along. A Spirit-filled husband and a Spirit-filled wife will get along. A Spirit-filled employer and a Spirit-filled employee will get along. Spirit-filled neighbors will get along. Spirit-filled church members will get along. The early Christians were Spirit-filled.

Three times in the New Testament, wine and the Holy Spirit were used in the same connection. John the Baptist was not to drink wine (see Luke 7:33), but to be filled with the Spirit. On the day of Pentecost, the Christians were accused of being drunk on new wine when they were filled with the Spirit (see Acts 2:13–18). Ephesians 5:18 says, "Be not drunk with wine, wherein is excess; but be filled with the Spirit."

Wine changes a person's face; so does the Holy Spirit. Wine changes a person's talk; so does the Holy Spirit. Wine changes a person's walk; so does the Holy Spirit. A man drunk on wine creates a commotion—and so does a man filled with the Spirit!

A Christian Has a Singing Heart

Finally, every Christian ought to be a singing Christian. "Speaking to yourselves in psalms and hymns and spiritual songs, singing and making melody in your heart to the Lord" (Eph. 5:19). The psalmist said, "Thy statutes have been my songs in the house of my pilgrimage" (Ps. 119:54).

The trouble with Christianity today and with so much of the church is that we've got the words, but we don't have the music. There is no melody to it. We have the mandates but not the melody. The law book is not a songbook. We've lost our song.

I have seen student musicians studying under the great masters. These masters insist on perfection. I listened to a student play the cello, and the young man played perfectly, or so I thought. But the old master said, "The trouble with you is, you're playing the notes but not the music."

You know what he meant? There's no life in it; there's no soul in it; he was just sawing away. He got it perfectly, yes; every note was right, but it was hollow.

How much of our worship is like that? We perform; everything is perfect. The ushers move like clockwork; the preacher doesn't miss a word; the music is flawless, but they've only got the notes and not the music. The statutes have not become songs.

If we ever get the song back into our worship, something will happen. The hallelujahs have gone out of our churches. If amens were ten dollars apiece, they wouldn't be any scarcer than they are today.

The Value of Emotion

I recall a story about a fellow who liked what he heard from one preacher's sermon and gave a hearty "Amen!" The usher went to him and said, "What's the matter?"

He said, "I got religion."

The usher said, "You didn't get it here."

May the Lord deliver us from the spiritual coldness that is in a lot of churches. We ought to have a song in our hearts.

We've got a prejudice against emotion today. What would anything be worth without emotion?

What would patriotism be worth without emotion? During World War I, Caruso, the great tenor, came to Atlanta and put on a concert. The last thing he sang was "The Star-Spangled Banner." When he hit the last note, he hit it an octave high with that voice of his. Probably no greater voice has ever been put in the throat of a human being. And it took thirty minutes to get that crowd quiet. Emotion!

What would love be worth without emotion? If you are a married man, let me ask you: when you proposed, did you go on a strictly business basis? Did you say, "Woman, I bring you two premises and a conclusion: first premise, marriage is a desirable institution; second premise, I have decided you'd be a suitable companion; I now come to my conclusion"? You know what she'd have said to your premises? "Get off the premises!"

And she ought to have said it. Those whose religion consists of "two premises and a conclusion" don't have any love or joy. They've got their theology right, and their chronology right, but they don't have any doxology!

I thank God I grew up in an old country church where old-fashioned revivals used to get tangled up with your heartstrings and your tear glands. You could tell when you had a revival then.

That was before some little professor got up in school and said, "As man increases intellectually, his emotional expression decreases." That same man goes to a football game and loses his hat, loses his head, and loses his voice yelling. He yells like a Comanche Indian at a football game and sits like a wooden Indian in church on Sunday morning.

Charles Finney said, "You'll never have a revival till Mr. Amen and Mr. Wet Eyes are in the congregation." I believe that. It's more than emotion, but it's not less.

Have You Got a Song in Your Heart?

When Jesus was in the temple, the little children were waving palm branches and folks were coming in lame and going out leaping, and they came in blind and went out seeing, and everybody was having a great time—except the Pharisees. They were standing over in the corner, and they didn't like it. They said, "Too much excitement."

They said to Jesus, "Hearest thou what these say?" These kids were making too much racket! Jesus said, "Yea; have ye never read, Out of the mouths of babes and sucklings thou hast perfected praise?" (Matt. 21:16).

A revival is when childish folks become childlike. "Heartfelt religion"—you don't hear that old phrase much anymore.

I think of a Christian man who worked in the mining district. Somebody went to look for him one day, and they were told, "He's way down in the mine somewhere, but he won't be hard to find; he'll be singing."

When they found him, he was singing that old song, "Beulah Land." And he had just come to the line that says, "Here shines undimmed one blissful day, / and all my night has passed away."[5] He was way down in the dark, but he had a light on the inside.

You'd better get a light on the inside, friend. The lights are all going out in this world. You'd better get a light that'll stand the darkness.

How many of these marks of a Bible-believing Christian do you have? Have you got a song in your heart?

Vance Havner: Enjoying the Desires of His Heart

(1982 *Proclaim Magazine* Interview)

In 1982, four years before Vance Havner went home to be with the Lord, Dennis Hester interviewed him from his home in Greensboro, North Carolina. At seventy-nine, Havner was still continuing to stir revival fires among God's people from coast to coast. During this interview, Havner took the time to laugh, reflect on his ministry, and encourage his fellow preachers.

Hester: How has preaching changed during your life?

Havner: Circumstances change, but preaching never changes. We preach a message so much greater than ourselves. We must give it our best as we stand behind the pulpit.

I hear so much today about tension. If the preacher is going to give preaching his best, he needs to be tense. I don't mean nervous, but keyed up with God's power and message. There's not anything that can rejuvenate me like preaching. Preaching should be full of life. It is life.

R.G. Lee used to say, "There's not anything wrong with me that a good sermon won't cure."

Hester: How do you prepare yourself and your sermons to preach?

Havner: I don't have a set pattern. I like to do a lot of walking and thinking. Walking is a thing of the past.

Preachers are involved in too many meetings and programs. Meditation and solitude are lacking in many of our preachers. Not so much praying, but just thinking about the things of God.

I have a place down the road where I do a lot of walking and thinking. Occasionally, I get distracted by someone on a bicycle or a jogger. I like to tell the story about the man who had a heart attack jogging from a health food store. You can't do much thinking while jogging and gasping for breath!

Hester: What do you see as the future of preaching?

Havner: There'll always be preaching. Preaching has been my priority for years. When I first began serving a church, I thought it was my duty to be of service to every club, social gathering, or committee that demanded my time and energy.

In my early days during revival meetings, I would overly commit myself during the day, speaking and visiting. Then that night, when the main service came, I was already worn out. I think visiting and preparation for a revival is the pastor's job, not the evangelist's. Now I limit my preaching to one service per day. I don't overeat or over-socialize after the meeting. Charles Finney spoke of these two evils, overeating and over-socializing.

Hester: What techniques of evangelism have proven successful for you?

Havner: I don't have any special techniques. I never have. I don't maneuver any preaching engagements. I've never done any advertising, printed brochures, or publicity. I am not an evangelist or a pastor, just a preacher. I've been trying for a long time.

There never was a time when I felt I shouldn't be preaching. I began preaching in 1913 at the age of twelve. I have more to do at the age of seventy-nine than I've ever had. I tell church folk that when I get a little older, I am going to have to cut down on the program.

I do a lot of Bible conferences. Preachers ask me how to get started in this type of work. I can't tell them how. It just happens. God calls you, and then He'll open the doors for you to preach. He'll make a way if He's called you. You just be there.

Hester: What do you think are the major strengths and weaknesses among Southern Baptist preachers today?

Havner: I think Southern Baptists have some good, strong preachers today. I've been on the platform with many of them. They are doing a great work, especially some of the younger ones.

Hester: You've met a lot of the spiritual giants of yesterday, haven't you?

Havner: Yes, I've been fortunate enough to hear some of the best teachers and preachers of this age and the past—such men as Billy Sunday, W.B. Riley, H.A. Ironside, J. Wilbur Chapman, Mel Trotter, Homer Rodeheaver, Gipsy Smith, George W. Truett, Baxter McLendon (known as "Cyclone

Mack"), James M. Gray, J. Gresham Machen, Donald Grey Barnhouse, Charles M. Alexander, William Jennings Bryan, and R.A. Torrey.

Hester: How would you suggest a person prepare for the preaching ministry?

Havner: First of all, there must be a genuine call from God. If you don't have that, you might as well forget it. We have too many folks that preach for publicity and money.

I can't say one doesn't need an education. The trouble with many schools today is you don't get enough Bible. The Bible must be a first in a preacher's life. We need more prophets today, not just the predicting type, but the "Thus saith the Lord" type. We need preachers that will take to the woods and spend time with God and His Word.

Hester: As you travel from coast to coast preaching, how much of an interest is there in revival?

Havner: There's not much interest in the spiritual life. I don't think America is ready for a revival, nor does she really want a revival. Like the Laodicean church in Revelation, she's neither cold nor hot. I see revival taking place in a few churches on a small scale. Of course, revival could take place in a massive way. We must remember, revival is always possible when people humble themselves, pray, seek God's face, and turn from their wicked ways. But too many churches are settled and satisfied.

Hester: How did your writing ministry begin?

Havner: Once again, there's no set pattern on how to get started. There's got to be fire in your bones. With God's help, it'll happen. I started writing devotions and drawing in the first grade. Later, I began writing an inspirational column called "Havner's Reflections." Little did I know as I wrote for the *Charlotte Observer*, the leading newspaper in North Carolina, that God was preparing me for a writing ministry. My first book, *By the Still Waters*, was published in 1934 and is still selling today. I've written articles for numerous publications and thirty-one books consisting of sermons, devotions, and collections of a variety of memorable experiences. One in that list was sort of an autobiography entitled, *Three Score and Ten*.

Douglas White did a biography of me a few years ago entitled, *Vance Havner: Journey from Jugtown*, and Baker Book Company has recently reprinted in paperback, *The Best of Vance Havner*.

I remember one book I wrote called *Blood, Bread and Fire*; the publishers felt it needed a new title. I never did like the new title because it read more like an epitaph than a book title. There it was in bold print: *Entered into Rest: Vance Havner.*

I get letters from all over the country telling me how my books have been a great comfort to troubled souls. That's worth the writing. All I've ever wanted to do was be a traveling preacher and write. God has given me the desires of my heart.

Hester: Out of the thirty-one books you've written, which one means the most to you and why?

Havner: *Though I Walk through the Valley* is special because I wrote the book in 1973 after the death of my wife, Sarah.

Sarah was a wonderful wife. So many youngsters are marrying today without love, romance, or any devotion for one another. I wasn't married until I was thirty-nine, but I am sure I got the woman God wanted me to have. Sarah was worth waiting for.

Hester: Do you have something you would like to say to your fellow ministers who will be reading this interview?

Havner: No better instruction is possible than Paul's words to Timothy. He emphasized: (1) doctrine—"Give attendance . . . to doctrine" (1 Tim. 4:13); (2) dynamic—"Stir up the gift of God, which is in thee" (2 Tim. 1:6); and (3) discipline—"Endure hardness, as a good soldier of Jesus Christ" (2 Tim. 2:3).

Always a Fresh Word from the Lord

(Biographical Sketch of Vance Havner: *Confident Living*, November 1987)

IT HAS BEEN SAID, "The trouble with the old school of the prophets is that the old fellows are gone, but not forgotten; and the trouble with today's preachers is that we are forgotten, but not gone."

On August 12, 1986, Dr. Vance Havner, one of America's most beloved preachers, went home to be with the Lord, whom he served for more than seventy years.

Havner is gone, but he shall never be forgotten. His powerful preaching comforted us when we felt afflicted and afflicted us when we became comfortable with the demands of Christ. His clever and humorous way of turning a phrase, and his ability to communicate deep spiritual truths in his homespun fashion with clarity and conviction, will always stick with us.

When so many preachers are trying to be "everything to everybody," Havner was satisfied with being who God created him to be—himself. Havner wasn't disappointed that he wasn't a "jack-of-all trades," but neither did he boast in what he did best: preach. Like the Old Testament prophet Jeremiah, Havner was created and destined to preach. He said on many occasions, "I've never known a time that I didn't feel called to be a preacher. All I've ever wanted to do was to preach all over this country and write books. And God has given me the desires of my heart."

Havner trusted Christ as his Savior at the age of ten and was baptized in South Fork River in the Backwoods of Vale, "Jugtown," North Carolina. He was licensed to preach at age twelve by Corinth Baptist Church of Vale and was ordained at age fifteen. It was an awesome experience for a boy of twelve to stand on a chair at First Baptist Church of Shelby, North Carolina, and preach to a congregation of 1000!

As Havner began preaching, he often heard scoffers say, "Boy preachers never last." In spite of the critics, Havner continued preaching, later serving as a pastor. He traveled countless miles as an itinerant preacher and delivered more than 13,000 sermons during his seventy-two years as a minister of the Word. Havner often referred to the comment about boy preachers not lasting, and with a grin he would say, "I think I've given it a pretty good try." Havner was still actively preaching at age eighty-two, but had done little preaching two years before his death because of ill health and two broken hips.

Havner took a different route from most ministers to prepare himself for his preaching and writing ministry. He never stayed anywhere long enough to graduate. He attended Boiling Springs High School (now Gardner-Webb College, where he was conferred the honorary degree of Doctor of Divinity in 1971), Wake Forest Baptist College (now a University), Catawba College, Moody Bible Institute and Florida Bible Institute.

Some evangelists may have considered Havner unorthodox because the only form of advertising Havner ever remembers using was in 1924 when he placed an ad in the *Biblical Recorder*, his home state's denominational newspaper. He simply stated that he was available to serve as a pastor. Havner was then called to his first pastorate, the Salem Baptist Church, for one year.

After resigning and returning to his old home place in the foothills of North Carolina, he preached in the surrounding area and, as Havner put it, "floundered trying to find my way."

Havner returned to serve the Salem Baptist Church a second time for three years. The little country congregation could tell their pastor was a different man, who had matured emotionally and spiritually. Havner commented on his second installment at Salem Baptist Church in his book *Threescore and Ten*.

> I stayed upstairs in a plain home, studied by a kerosene lamp, drank water from a pitcher and warmed by a wood burning stove; but I put in three years of the best Bible study I have ever done. God honors the study and preaching of His Word. Pity the preacher who uses a text only as a launching platform from which to blast off into space, departing therefrom and never returning thereto! There is a power in the direct preaching of the Bible that attends no other pulpit exercise.[1]

Havner's next divine appointment was to pastor the First Baptist Church in Charleston, South Carolina. Scott Walker served as an associate pastor when Havner was pastor in Charleston. Walker said of Havner, "Havner never was fond of many of the pastoral duties other than preaching. He'd have me to do all of the weddings, funerals, and baptisms. Havner was a prophet; all he wanted to do was preach."

The congregation eventually became concerned about the amount of time their young evangelist-pastor was spending attending revivals and Bible conferences. Havner stayed at the oldest Baptist Church in the South for five years. He then decided his time had come to launch out on faith and venture into the traveling ministry he had envisioned from boyhood.

Havner began his new ministry in 1940. His first meetings were to be held with the Mel Trotter Mission in Grand Rapids, Michigan. He got as far as Chicago, where he came down with the flu and had to be hospitalized. It would become Havner's custom to migrate toward Florida to preach during the winter, but at this particular time, as Havner battled the flu in the North, the South's "land of sunshine" looked especially inviting.

So Havner rearranged his schedule and accepted an invitation to preach in a Bible conference at the Florida Bible Institute in Tampa. As Havner recuperated, he met two people who would become enduring friends. One was the would-be evangelist, Billy Graham, who was a student at the Bible school. The other person was Miss Sara Allred, the dean of women and the manager of the bookstore.

Miss Allred nursed Havner back to health with chicken soup, a game of dominoes before a big open fire, and long strolls in the Florida sunshine and moonlight. When Havner left to resume his speaking schedule, the love and letters of Sara Allred followed him. They were married in December, 1940. They set out together in the itinerant ministry, for which, Havner said, "I was now far better prepared." Sara did all of Havner's driving. Havner never got a driver's license and was 66 before he purchased an automobile!

Havner was nearly forty years old when he married. He lived with Sara, his companion and coworker, for thirty-three years. In 1973, she was struck with a dreaded disease that distorted her lovely features and rendered her a helpless invalid.

As Havner struggled with the suffering and death of his beloved Sara, he wrote what became his all-time best seller, *Though I Walk through the Valley*. In this intimate book, Havner reflected upon the waiting, suffering, loneliness and grief during the nightmare of losing his beloved Sara. He also testified to the peace and love of God that sustained him. *Hope Thou in God* followed in 1977 and is a continuation of Havner's struggles and victories as he adjusted to living without Sara.

"It took me nearly forty years to get married," said Havner, "but Sara was worth the wait. I loved her so much. People getting married today don't believe in romance like Sara and I did. All they believe in today is sex."

As I became better acquainted with Havner through his preaching and his thirty-six books, and as I visited with him in his home in Greensboro, one supreme characteristic stands out above all the rest: Havner was a holy man of God. Dr. Alton H. McEachern, Havner's pastor at First Baptist Church of Greensboro, appropriately described Havner as one who was "intensely spiritual, but perfectly natural."

Havner nurtured his spiritual nature by rising early in the morning and strolling in the woods to reflect on the things of God and to watch birds. There was nothing mystical about bird watching, but only a habit Havner began as a boy and continued all of his life. Havner referred to nature often in his writings and found a joy in identifying countless birds by their color and song. The wood thrush was his favorite.

"Meditation is a lost art among most preachers today," said Havner. "They're too busy, wrapped up with programs and committee meetings. I'm always calling preachers to more meditation, reflection, and solitude within this rat race in which we live. If we don't come apart to be with the Lord, we will surely come apart."

Havner was a free spirit as God used him like a sword to proclaim the truth with power and purpose. This "old-time" revivalist never relied on trends or slogans to convict people to love or to serve Jesus. Like a prophet of old, Havner always had a fresh "word from the Lord" that did the convicting and changing.

"We don't need to be in the novelty shop as much as we need to be in the antique shop where we find the old truths of God's Word," said Havner. "We don't need something new today half as much as we need something so old that it would be new if anybody tried it."

There's no way this side of heaven to estimate the eternal good and undying challenge Havner's prophet messages from pulpit and pen have brought to God's people across our country. He faithfully honored God by courageously speaking to our age, convicting our hearts, revealing our sins, and pointing to "Jesus only" as the remedy.

From a humble beginning in the foothills of the Blue Ridge Mountains, Vance Havner became one of America's best-loved and most-quoted preachers and authors. Churches from various denominations, in addition to his own Southern Baptist Convention, are indebted to Havner for stirring revival fires in hearts of clergy and laity alike. But, with all his success and recognition, he never considered himself to be anything but a servant of the Lord Jesus Christ.

About the Compiler and Editor

DENNIS HESTER BECAME a life-long Vance Havner fan after hearing Havner speak at Gardner-Webb College, where he was a freshman, in 1972. Hester has pastored churches in North Carolina, South Carolina, and Virginia. He has also served as a chaplain, revivalist, and volunteer missionary.

He is the author of numerous articles and newspaper columns and has compiled four books on Vance Havner: *The Vance Havner Quotebook*, *The Vance Havner Notebook*, *Sermon Sparklers by Vance Havner* (all published by Baker Book House), and *When God Breaks Through, Revival Sermons by Vance Havner*, published by Kregel Publications.

Dennis and his wife Pam make their home in Winston-Salem, NC. They have two grown children, Nathan and Rachael and a companion Labrador Retriever named Falco.

For speaking engagements and church consulting in how to resolve and manage conflict and how to keep your church healthy, you may contact Rev. Hester at:

Dennis@Dennishester.com

Notes

Chapter 2

1. Harold Lillenas, "Wonderful, Wonderful, Jesus Is to Me" (hymn), public domain.
2. Elizabeth A. Allen, "Rock Me to Sleep" (hymn), public domain.
3. William Ralph Featherstone, "My Jesus I Love Thee" (hymn), public domain.

Chapter 3

1. Selected, "Behind in His Reading" (poem), from John R. Rice, compiler and editor, *742 Heart-Warming Poems* (Murfreesboro, TN: Sword of the Lord Publications, 1964), #479.

Chapter 4

1. John H. Sammis, "Trust and Obey" (hymn), public domain.

Chapter 6

1. John Gneisenau Neihardt, "Battle Cry" (poem). Reprinted by permission of the John G. Neihardt Trust.
2. Martha Snell Nicholson, "His Plan for Me" (poem), public domain.

Chapter 7

1. Elizabeth C. Clephane, "Beneath the Cross of Jesus" (hymn), 1868, public domain.
2. Old folk song with varying lyrics, author unknown.
3. Ray Palmer, "My Faith Looks Up to Thee" (hymn), 1830, public domain.

Chapter 8

1. John Henry Jowett, "The Perils of the Preacher," The Expositor, vol. XV, no. 1, p. 3. From a lecture on the Lyman Beecher Foundation at Yale, and published in *The Preacher: His Life and Work* (New York: Geo. H. Doran Co., 1912).
2. Johnson Oatman, Jr., "Higher Ground" (hymn), public domain.

Chapter 9

1. Daniel Webster, "An anniversary address delivered before the federal gentlemen of Concord, July 4, 1806 [in commemoration of American independence]" (Concord, NH: George Hough, 1806), 7.
2. Samuel Stennet, "On Jordan's Stormy Banks I Stand" (hymn), 1787, public domain.

Chapter 10

1. George Bennard, "The Old Rugged Cross" (hymn), 1913, public domain.
2. William R. Featherstone, "My Jesus, I Love Thee" (hymn), 1864, public domain.
3. Adelaide A. Pollard, "Have Thine Own Way, Lord" (hymn), 1906, public domain.
4. Frances R. Havergal, "Take My Life and Let It Be" (hymn), 1874, public domain.
5. Edgar Page Stites, "Beulah Land" (hymn), 1876, public domain.

Always a Fresh Word from the Lord

1. Vance Havner, *Threescore and Ten* (Ada, MI: Revell, 1973), 42.

This book is published by CLC Publications, an outreach of CLC Ministries International. The purpose of CLC is to make evangelical Christian literature available to all nations so that people may come to faith and maturity in the Lord Jesus Christ. We hope this book has been life changing and has enriched your walk with God through the work of the Holy Spirit. If you would like to know more about CLC, we invite you to visit our website:

www.clcusa.org

To know more about the remarkable story of the founding of CLC International, we encourage you to read

LEAP OF FAITH

Norman Grubb

Paperback
Size 5¼ x 8, Pages 248
ISBN: 978-0-87508-650-7
ISBN (*e-book*): 978-1-61958-055-8

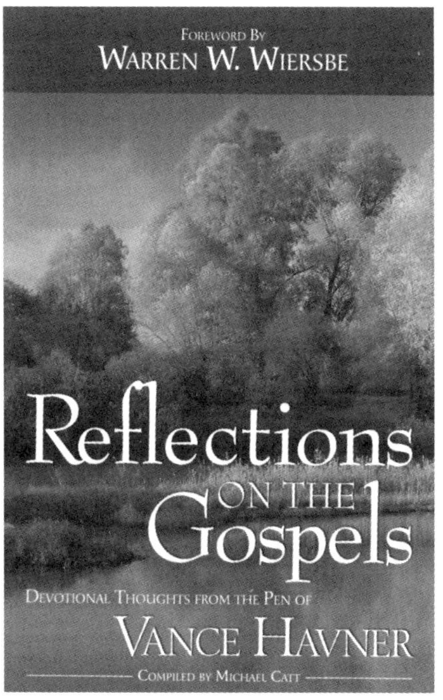

REFLECTIONS ON THE GOSPELS

Vance Havner (compiled by Michael C. Catt)

Vance Havner's *Reflections on the Gospels* was rescued by Michael Catt from a collection of newspaper columns and compiled for the first time into book form. The result is a wonderful devotional volume that gives a unique insight into God's Word through the eyes of this great preacher.

Paperback
Size 5¼ x 8, Pages 227
ISBN: 978-0-87508-783-3
ISBN (*e-book*): 978-1-936143-42-9

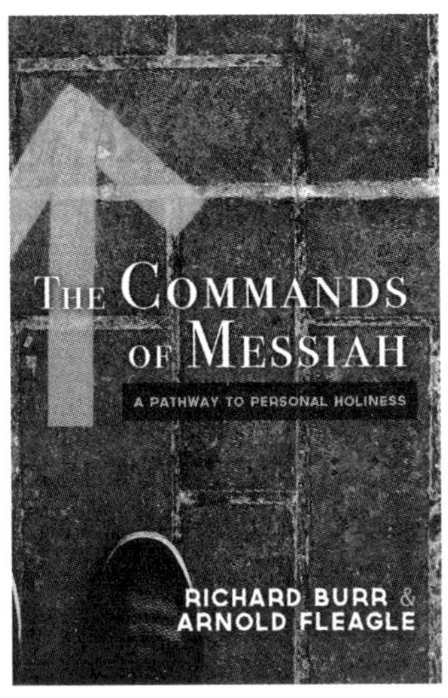

THE COMMANDS OF MESSIAH

Richard Burr and Arnold Fleagle

Many Christians admit to feeling somewhat intimidated by the subject of holiness and Christlike living, but the expectation from Scripture is undeniably clear. Burr and Fleagle argue that the open secret to growing in the image of Christ lies in obedience to his commands. Using an encouraging, guilt-free approach that avoids any tendency toward legalism, the authors discuss eleven specific commands given by Jesus and show how believers can fulfill them in the power of the Holy Spirit.

Paperback
Size 5¼ x 8, Pages 154
ISBN: 978-1-61958-319-1
ISBN (*e-book*): 978-1-61958-320-7

UPGRADE

Michael Catt

In *Upgrade,* Michael Catt outlines the behaviors and mindsets of immature faith and explains how God equips and empowers us to enjoy the Christ-filled life promised to us in the Epistles. Catt challenges us to accept the "upgrade" offered in Scripture to all Christians through the guidance of the Holy Spirit.

Paperback
Size 5¼ x 8, Pages 177
ISBN: 978-1-936143-21-4
ISBN (*e-book*): 978-1-936143-92-4

ANOTHER CHANCE AT LIFE

Warren W. Wiersbe

Have you made a mess of your circumstances? Jesus told a story about such a person—and the answer lay in his loving and forgiving father. If you've come to the end of yourself—or simply need a reminder of God's grace and love—this book is for you.

Paperback
Size 5 1/4 x 8, Pages 88
ISBN: 978-0-87508-996-6

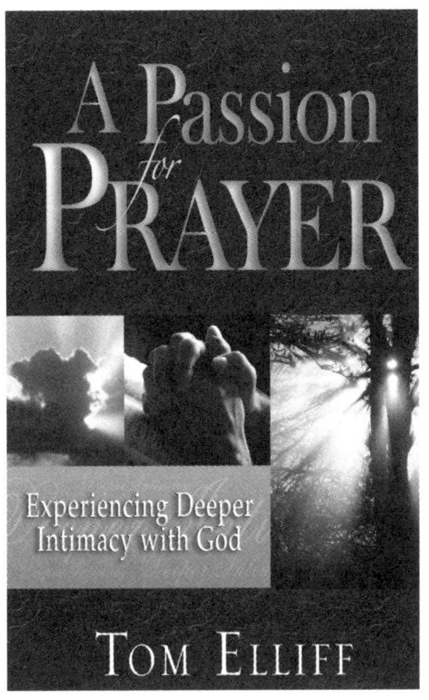

A PASSION FOR PRAYER

Tom Elliff

Of all the disciplines of the Christian life, prayer is perhaps the most neglected. Yet Jesus' brief earthly life was permeated with it. *A Passion for Prayer* seeks to help you develop—or deepen—your communion with God. Drawing on personal experience and God's Word, Pastor Tom Elliff shares principles for daily coming before the throne of grace.

Paperback
Size 5 1/4 x 8, Pages 252
ISBN: 978-1-936143-03-0
ISBN (*e-book*): 978-1-936143-26-9